There's a Mystery There

Also by Jonathan Cott

Susan Sontag: The Complete Rolling Stone *Interview*

Days That I'll Remember: Spending Time with John Lennon and Yoko Ono

Dinner with Lenny: The Last Long Interview with Leonard Bernstein

On the Sea of Memory: A Journey from Forgetting to Remembering

Back to a Shadow in the Night: Music Writings and Interviews: 1968–2001

Homelands (Poems)

Thirteen: A Journey into the Number

Isis and Osiris

Wandering Ghost: The Odyssey of Lafcadio Hearn

Visions and Voices

The Search for Omm Sety

Conversations with Glenn Gould

Dylan

Pipers at the Gates of Dawn: The Wisdom of Children's Literature

Forever Young

City of Earthly Love (Poems)

He Dreams What Is Going on Inside His Head: Ten Years of Writing

Stockhausen: Conversations with the Composer

There's a Mystery There

THE PRIMAL VISION OF MAURICE SENDAK

Jonathan Cott

DOUBLEDAY

New York   London   Toronto   Sydney   Auckland

www.doubleday.com

DOUBLEDAY and the portrayal of an anchor with a dolphin are
registered trademarks of Penguin Random House LLC.

Book design by Maria Carella
Jacket image from *Outside Over There*. Used by permission of HarperCollins Publishers.
Jacket design by Michael J. Windsor

Grateful acknowledgment is made to Coleman Barks for permission to reprint
an excerpt of "Quatrain 91" by Rumi, translated by Coleman Barks,
from *Open Secret* (Threshold Books, 1986).

Library of Congress Cataloging-in-Publication Data
Names: Cott, Jonathan, author.
Title: There's a mystery there : the primal vision of Maurice Sendak / Jonathan Cott.
Description: First edition. | New : Doubleday, [2017]
Identifiers: LCCN 2016050812 (print) | LCCN 2016055152 (ebook) | ISBN 9780385540438
(hardcover) | ISBN 9780385540445 (ebook)
Subjects: LCSH: Sendak, Maurice—Criticism and interpretation. | Children—Books and
reading—United States—History—20th century. | Children's stories, American—History and
criticism. | Children's stories, American—Illustrations. | BISAC: LITERARY CRITICISM
/ American / General. | BIOGRAPHY & AUTOBIOGRAPHY / Literary. | LITERARY
CRITICISM / General.
Classification: LCC PS3569.E6 Z65 2017 (print) | LCC PS3569.E6 (ebook) |
DDC 813/.54—dc23
LC record available at https://lccn.loc.gov/2016050812

MANUFACTURED IN GERMANY

1   3   5   7   9   10   8   6   4   2

First Edition

In memory of my brother, Jeremy Cott

We say "far away"; the Zulu people have a word for that which means "There where someone cries out: *O mother, I am lost.*"

—MARTIN BUBER, *I and Thou*

Each childhood is a night light in the bedroom of memories.

—GASTON BACHELARD, *The Poetics of Reverie*

Contents

There's a Mystery There

Introduction

"Genius," wrote the French poet Charles Baudelaire, "is only childhood recalled at will," and few creative artists' lives and works have given more credence to this notion than Maurice Sendak, who was, in the words of *The New York Times,* "widely considered to be the most important children's book artist of the twentieth century." Upon his death on May 8, 2012, at the age of eighty-three, *The New Yorker*'s Adam Gopnik declared that his passing was "a loss not only, or even primarily, to the world of children's books, but to the larger American literature of the imagination."

"I don't believe that, in a way, the kid I was grew up into me," Sendak confided to the writer Nat Hentoff in 1966. "He still exists somewhere, in the most graphic, plastic, physical way. I have a tremendous concern for him and interest in him. I communicate with him—or try to—all the time, and one of my worst fears is losing contact with him. And I don't want this to sound coy or schizophrenic," he added, "but at least once a day I feel I have to make contact. The pleasures I get as an adult are heightened by the fact that I experience them as a child at the same time. Like, when autumn comes, as an adult I welcome the departure of the heat, and simultaneously, as a child would, I start anticipating the snow and the first day it will be possible to use a sled. This dual apperception does break down occasionally, and that usually happens when my work is going badly. I get a sour feeling about books in general and my own in particular. The next stage is annoyance at my dependence on this dual apperception, and I reject it. Then I become depressed. When excitement about what I'm working on returns, so does the child, and we're on happy terms again."

The French philosopher Gaston Bachelard once remarked that "an excess of childhood is the germ of a poem," and in Sendak's case it was the catalyst for more than one hundred illustrated children's books that have sold more than thirty million copies in the United States alone. Among the earliest and most enduring of these are *A Hole Is To Dig,* for which Sendak provided mercurial pen-and-ink drawings of a gaggle of feisty, rollicking city kids that accompanied the poet Ruth Krauss's assemblage of children's definitions ("A face is so you can make faces," "A tablespoon is to eat a table with," "A dream is to look at the night and see things"); and the equally beloved Little Bear series, a quintet of Else Holmelund Minarik's tender easy-reader stories for which Sendak's understated, cross-hatched Victorian drawings memorably incarnated three generations of a snug and kind-hearted ursine family.

Mud is to jump in and slide in and yell doodleedoodleedoo

Anh-h-h-h!

ABOVE:
From *A Hole Is To Dig*

RIGHT:
From *Little Bear*

But in the sixteen books that he both wrote and illustrated himself, Sendak created some of his own indelible children's-literature immortals, among them the incorrigibly willful Pierre from the *Nutshell Library,* whose automatic "I don't care!" response to every parental request is a mantra that will forever resound wherever one encounters the terrible twos, the terrifying threes, and the fearsome fours; the precocious and preening young Brooklyn diva named Rosie from *The Sign on Rosie's Door,* who loves to array herself in her mother's and grandmother's clothes and accessories and then perform a myriad of tragic and comic roles for the "hurdy-gurdy, fantasy-plagued Brooklyn street kids"—as Sendak described them—who are her unwaveringly loyal fans; the irrepressible little boy named Mickey from *In the Night Kitchen,* who floats out of his bed and out of his pajamas and then free-falls, completely naked, into a surrealistic underworld kitchen where a trio of grinning Oliver Hardy look-alike bakers proceed to mix him into batter and try, unsuccessfully, to turn him into a delicious Mickey-Cake; and, most famous and infamous of them all, the rebellious wolf-suited Max from *Where the Wild Things Are,* who threatens to eat up his mom, is summarily banished to his room, conjures from his enraged imagination a pack of befanged and beclawed monsters, triumphs over them, and journeys back home to find a still-hot supper awaiting him.

Goethe famously remarked, "One must ask children and birds how cherries and strawberries taste," and it is children themselves who are the ultimate arbiters of who or who is not a children's-book hero for the ages. And for all of Sendak's commercial success and the innumerable awards and honors that he received during his lifetime, including the 2003 Astrid Lindgren Memorial Award, which is the children's-literature equivalent of the Nobel Prize, few things pleased him more than a card he received from a little boy named Jim that contained a charming drawing of a wild thing. "I answer all my

THERE'S A MYSTERY THERE

children's letters, sometimes very hastily," Sendak once explained, "but this one I lingered over, and I sent him my own card and drew my own picture of a wild thing on it, and I wrote: 'Dear Jim, I loved your card.' Then I got a letter back from his mother, and she said: 'Jim loved your card so much he ate it.' That to me was one of the highest compliments I've ever received. He didn't care that it was an original Maurice Sendak drawing or anything. He saw it, he loved it, he ate it." And that boy might well have been almost any one of Sendak's mettlesome (and hungry!) child heroes.

Of all the books that Sendak both wrote and illustrated, only two featured child heroines. One of them, of course, is Rosie, whom he based on a mesmerizing and indefatigable ten-year-old girl from his childhood Brooklyn neighborhood. He spent several months assiduously observing and making sketches of her through his parents' second-floor Brooklyn apartment window, and confessed, "I loved Rosie—she knew how to get through a day," asserting that "she was the child all of my future characters would be modeled on."

The other Sendak heroine is Ida, the fearless soul sister of Max and Mickey, who appears in *Outside Over There,* which was the third book of what he regarded as a picture-book trilogy that also included *Where the Wild Things Are* and *In the Night Kitchen.* He explained that all three were "variations on the same theme: how children master various feelings—anger, boredom, fear, frustration, jealousy—and manage to come to grips with the reality of their lives," and remarked that "over the longevity of a man's life and work you get a sense of where his mind is, where his heart is, where his humor is, where his dread is, and everything for me is in those three books."

Although *Outside Over There* is the least known of the three, Sendak stated that it was "the most personal of all my books, and my favorite," and declared it to be his masterpiece. And he was not alone in that assessment.

5

Upon its publication in 1981, Jerry Griswold, the children's-book scholar and former director of the National Center for the Study of Children's Literature, wrote: "*Outside Over There* is Sendak's best work so far. It marks the apogee of the picture-book form, a simply profound story told in incantatory words and color drawings of stunning beauty." And thirty-four years later, in 2015, the playwright Tony Kushner, who was a close friend and collaborator of Sendak's, commented, "For me, *Outside Over There* is Maurice's last completely successful great book, and with it he succeeded in his enormous balancing act, which was to take a medium that needed to speak to a very young and unformed audience and that at the same time allowed him to manifest the aesthetic expression of a very complicated, very adult intellect and soul. I think that in this book he takes it as far as it can go. This is the maximum degree that this medium of the children's picture book can contain of deep adult meaning, and the miracle of this book is that it works for both a young and a grown-up audience."

Outside Over There tells the story of nine-year-old Ida, whose father is away at sea and whose melancholic, emotionally unavailable mother is pining away in an arbor, leaving it up to Ida to look after her baby sister. One day, while playing her magic wonder horn, Ida turns her back on the baby, and during that moment of distraction two faceless, hooded goblins climb up a wooden ladder, sneak in through an open window, snatch the baby, and in her place substitute a changeling made of ice that, when Ida hugs it, melts in her arms. Enraged, Ida flies backward out the window in her mother's voluminous yellow rain cloak, but only when she turns herself around does she finally discover her sister imprisoned in the goblins' grotto. Ida blasts out a frenzied jig on her horn, and the shape-shifting goblins, whose cloaks fall away, revealing them to be naked babies, dissolve into a dancing stream. Noticing her crooning and clapping sister sitting in an enormous broken eggshell, Ida takes her in her arms, sets out on a path through the woods, and finally brings her sister back home safe and sound.

The plot of *Outside Over There* was one of the seminal inspirations for Jim Henson's 1986 cult fantasy film *Labyrinth,* in which a sixteen-year-old girl has to journey to the center of an immense otherworldly maze in order to rescue her infant brother from the clutches of a goblin king, and a copy of *Outside Over There* can be seen sitting on the heroine's bookshelf, alongside copies of *Where the Wild Things Are* and a volume of Grimms' fairy tales. And like all great fairy tales, *Outside Over There* has the simplicity of an elemental story and at the same time the mysteriousness, depth, and multiplicity of meanings of a dream, as we imaginatively descend with Ida into the underworld goblins' grotto, where what is outer becomes inner and where what has been lost is found. As Tony Kushner suggests, *Outside Over There* is a book for both a young and a grown-up audience, and when it was first published, Harper & Row sold and promoted it in both the children's and the adult book markets, which greatly pleased Sendak, who admitted, "I had waited a long time to be taken out of kiddie-book land and allowed to join the artists of America."

But Sendak, of course, still had one foot in that land, which, he informed us, was located "next to Neverneverville and Peterpanburg," and where censorious adult guardians were on permanent watch patrol. When *In the Night Kitchen* was first published, in 1971, some librarians who were disturbed by the frontal nudity of its little hero drew or painted diapers on Mickey in their libraries' copies of the book. (*Night Kitchen* has always ranked high on the American Library Association's list of frequently banned or challenged books.) And when *Where the Wild Things Are* first appeared, in 1963, the publisher received letters from librarians, educators, and parents who were concerned that the book might upset some children, induce nightmares, or, even worse, inspire them to challenge their mothers and create a rumpus at home. Conversely, the act of maternal deprivation disconcerted the child psychiatrist Bruno Bettelheim, who commented that "the basic anxiety of the child is desertion. To be sent to bed alone is one desertion, and without food is the second desertion. The combination is the worst desertion that can threaten a child." (Bettelheim, however, later admitted that he hadn't read the book when he made this comment and had only been told its plot; he would reverse his opinion a decade later.) But as a reviewer for the *Cleveland Press* contrarily suggested, "Boys and girls may have to shield their parents from this book. Parents are very easily scared."

There are some parents who have indeed been scared of *Outside Over There*. One of them complained, "Yikes! This book made my son afraid that goblins would steal him away in the night, and that babies might be goblins. Why on earth would you want to plant the idea of fear and worry with your children just before bedtime? Don't read this to your toddler/preschooler/school-age/tween/teenage kids!" But another parent saw it differently: "My mother refuses to read it to my girls, who are just-turned-two and almost-five," she reported, "but my girls, both of them, *adore* this book—they are enthralled by Ida's resourcefulness, her bravery, and the consequences of her initial carelessness—and it seems to speak to them on some deep level." And a third parent, speaking for herself, reflected, "I'm so glad that there exist children's books that are so puzzling and complex and you're never finished reading them. Even if the book troubles me in its vague, weird way, that kind of reaction from pictures and a couple hundred words of text is really quite remarkable. And I'm even glad that someone wanted to ban this one because otherwise I might not ever have read it."

. . .

A PERSONAL NOTE: I first met Maurice Sendak in 1976. For a long while I had been hoping to write a profile of him for *Rolling Stone* magazine, and when I telephoned him in early May of that year to ask if he might be willing to do an interview with me, he seemed hesitant. "I've just begun working on a new picture book," he told me, "so I'm not sure that this is the right time for an interview. But let me think about it, and I'll call you back and let you know one way or the other." I was hoping for the best, and when I received a phone call from him a week later, he confessed that he'd been having some trouble working on the text for his new book and wouldn't mind taking a break from it and had therefore decided that he would be glad to see me.

When I visited him at his home in Ridgefield, Connecticut, the following month, I asked him about his new work, and he informed me that it was going to be called *Outside Over There* and remarked, "This is going to be the last part of my trilogy, and of the three books this one will be the strangest. *Wild Things* now seems to me to be a very simple book—its simplicity is probably what made it successful, but I could never be that simple again. *Night Kitchen* I much prefer—it reverberates on double levels. But this third book will reverberate on triple levels. It's so dense already, and I don't know what it means, and I can't get beyond the first seven lines. But I'll get there. I feel it in me, like a woman having a baby."

Like many expectant mothers, Sendak didn't want to say too much at that time about the child-to-be. But over the course of our wide-ranging and revelatory conversation about his life, his work, and the fantasies and obsessions that drove his creative processes, he nevertheless touched on some of the images and themes from his previous books that would reappear in *Outside Over There*: naked babies, children in a rage, children flying and falling, absent parents, precarious journeys, reassuring homecomings, the music of Mozart, and the feeling of being outside and inside at one and the same time.

My profile of Sendak was published in the 1976 Christmas issue of *Rolling Stone,* whose cover displayed his original color drawing of a resplendent, ornament-bedecked Wild Things Christmas tree. Sendak and I stayed in touch, and over the next several years we occasionally met up for lunch or dinner, and we eventually collaborated on a book that presented examples of some of the glorious Victorian picture books for children created by artists such as Randolph Caldecott, Walter Crane, and Richard Doyle that had been seminal influences on his own work.

In March 1981, Sendak sent me an advance copy of *Outside Over There,* which was finally going to be published after its five-year gestation period,

Maurice Sendak's cover drawing for the December 30, 1976, issue of *Rolling Stone*

and when I asked him if he'd be willing to talk to me about the much antici-pated new arrival for a book that I was then in the process of writing about children's literature, he said he'd be happy to do so. "We spoke a little bit about *Outside Over There* five years ago," he reminded me, "and it took a while, but now it's here, and I have to tell you that when I was dreaming the book, what I was imagining was the most real thing I've ever felt, and it seemed to me as if nothing that would occur after it would be as real or so intensely wonderful."

But over the next three decades of his life, Sendak was involved with many other wonderful projects. He designed fantastical sets and costumes for operas and ballets by composers such as Mozart, Janàček, Ravel, Prokofiev, and Tchaikovsky; he worked with Spike Jonze and Dave Eggers on their film adaptation of *Where the Wild Things Are;* and he continued to illustrate remark-able books. He collaborated with Tony Kushner on an inspired picture-book retelling of Hans Krása's 1938 children's opera *Brundibár,* a work about two cou-rageous children who outwit a maleficent hurdy-gurdy grinder that had been performed fifty-five times by the children of Theresienstadt, a Nazi concen-tration camp. He used two Mother Goose nursery rhymes as the springboard for his corruscating *We Are All in the Dumps with Jack and Guy,* a picture book that takes place at the height of the AIDS epidemic, about a homeless black child who is kidnapped by a gang of rats and then saved by two boys named Jack and Guy, with the assistance of a gigantic cat and a luminous, protective, maternal moon. He provided the illustrations for *Dear Mili,* a desolate fairy tale about a lost motherless child by Wilhelm Grimm, and he created astonishing, sexually charged watercolor drawings for Herman Melville's novel *Pierre* and Heinrich von Kleist's play *Penthesilea,* both of which were intended for an adult readership. And he even appeared in the HBO television film of Kushner's *Angels in America,* playing a rabbi in a scene with Meryl Streep.

ABOVE: From *Brundibar*; BELOW: From *We Are All in the Dumps with Jack and Guy*

From *Dear Mili*

After *Outside Over There,* however, Sendak both wrote and illustrated only two picture books. *Bumble-Ardy,* which was published in 2011, a year before his death, is a high-spirited but mordant comedy about an orphaned pig—his parents, we're told, "gorged and gained weight and got ate"—who decides to throw himself a costume party in his Aunt Adeline's house to celebrate his ninth birthday. He invites some of his brine-imbibing swine pals,

ABOVE:
From *Bumble-Ardy*

RIGHT:
From *My Brother's Book*:
"Jack and Guy, two brothers,
dreaming the same dream"

who proceed to raise a wild-pigs rumpus until Adeline returns home and admonishes her nephew: "Okay, smarty, you've had your party, but never again," to which Bumble-Ardy forebodingly replies, "I promise! I swear! I won't ever turn ten!"

Sendak's last completed picture book, *My Brother's Book,* was published posthumously in 2013 and tells the apocalyptic story of two inseparable brothers, once again named Jack and Guy, who are "dreaming the same dream" until a blazing star smashes into the earth, catapulting Jack to a world of ice and Guy into the stomach of a bear. But on the book's final page we see them once again united, enfolded in each other's arms, as Guy whispers to Jack, "Good night, / And you will dream of me."

WITH ITS RADIANT, visionary, Blake-inspired watercolor drawings, *My Brother's Book* is a heartbreaking, elegiac testament to Sendak's abiding, illimitable love for his own brother, Jack—"I don't believe in an afterlife," he told Terry Gross on her radio show *Fresh Air* eight months before he died, "but I still fully expect to see my brother again"—and is a profoundly affecting and self-revealing work. But of all Sendak's picture books, it seems to me that *Outside Over There* is ultimately the one that most fully expresses and illuminates the complex and manifold nature of his creative being, and I believe that to understand *Outside Over There* is in large part to understand Sendak himself.

Because he considered *Outside Over There* to be his most personal book, I begin *There's a Mystery There* with an account of Sendak's Polish-Jewish immigrant family, his Brooklyn childhood, his apprenticeship as a children's-book illustrator, and the private associations and obsessions that found their way into this book, in particular his lifelong fixation on the kidnapping in

1932 of Charles Lindbergh, Jr., the infant son of Charles and Anne Morrow Lindbergh, an event that traumatized Sendak when he was three and a half years old and that he avowed was the key that could unlock the secret meaning of *Outside Over There*.

I also write about some of the most significant of his works that preceded this book, most especially *Where the Wild Things Are* and *In the Night Kitchen*. Upon completing the first of these, Sendak confessed, "*Wild Things* was a personal exorcism, and in it I went deeper into my childhood than anything I'd done before, and I must go deeper in the ones to come," and he confided to a friend that *Night Kitchen* "came from the direct middle of me, and it hurt like hell extracting it. Yes, indeed, very birth-delivery-type pains, and it's as regressed as I imagine I can go." But he in fact went further, and later described *Outside Over There* as "the picture book that is the last excavation of my soul, the last archeological Sendakian dig," stating that it had required him to "plummet as far down deep into myself as I could go."

In order to explore the complex psychological, visual, and literary depths and mysteries of *Outside Over There*—and to gain multiple perspectives on this intricate and multifaceted book in the context of Sendak's life and work—I turned for assistance to four companion guides: the psychoanalyst Richard M. Gottlieb, the Jungian analyst Margaret Klenck, the art historian and children's-book scholar Jane Doonan, and Tony Kushner. In *There's a Mystery There* I present my conversations with them, as well as my own discussion with Sendak himself, about the book that he called "the most painful experience of my creative life" but that he always considered to be his greatest triumph. "The picture book is my battleground," Sendak once declared, adding, "It's where I consolidate my powers and put them together in what I hope is a legitimate, viable form that is meaningful to somebody else and not just to me. It's where I put down those fantasies that have been with me all of my life and where I give them a form that means something. I live inside the picture book; that's where I fight my battles, and where I hope to win my wars."

Part One

Maurice Sendak, the youngest of three children of Philip and Sarah Sendak, was born in Brooklyn on June 10, 1928, when his sister, Natalie, was nine and his brother, Jack, was five. As Philip would later describe Maurice's delivery, "Dr. Brummer said the child would not have a natural birth. The doctor put his instruments in a big pot and boiled them. With the tongs he took the little head and turned it, and Maurice came out all by himself. That was the only time that I saw how a child is born. Maurice's laugh was a little bell."

Philip and Sarah had come to New York before World War I from

Sarah Sendak with Jack, infant
Maurice, and Natalie (1928)

Jewish shtetls in Poland. Philip had crossed the Atlantic in pursuit of a girl. "The girl was a scandal," Maurice would tell the children's-book historian Leonard Marcus, "and everyone paid to put her on a ship and get her out of sight. So she went to America, and my father then drove his siblings and parents crazy because he wanted money to go on the next ship because he said he couldn't live without her. My grandparents refused to help—they cursed and disowned him and said the prayer for the dead. But his sisters and brother collected the money he needed, and so he followed this girl to New York. But when he got there just three weeks later, he found out that she had already married somebody else, and that she had a delicatessen on West Eighty-Seventh Street and Broadway! So he went to see her and he said, 'What's the matter with you! You got married to this Shlomo here?'

And she said, 'Philip, Philip, don't worry! Nothing's changed!' Later she and my mother became very good friends, and I always wondered if my mother knew the whole story. I adored her. Unlike my mother, she was a very giving, very emotional woman. Plus—free hot dogs! I can see myself rushing into her arms and feeling how big and warm her breasts were and how delicious she smelled, of hot dogs and knishes and everything. Come on, I loved her!"

Sarah—who was always called Sadie—was the eldest daughter of an impoverished Talmudic scholar and was sent to America when she was just sixteen, after the death of her father, in order to earn enough money to bring over her relatives. (Philip's entire family remained in Poland, and none of them survived the Holocaust.) Sadie had been told that a pushcart dealer and his wife would rent her a room, but shortly after she arrived, the man was killed in an automobile accident, so she survived by working in sweatshops. She met Philip at the wedding of a man who had also immigrated to America from her Polish village. Upon hearing her read aloud a story by Sholem Aleichem, Philip was immediately smitten and introduced himself to her. "After that," he recalled, "I courted her every Saturday and Sunday, and we went to City Hall in the Bronx for a marriage license."

Philip was a dressmaker who, along with two partners, had a shop called Lucky Stitching in Manhattan. Childhood photographs show Natalie attired in velvet and Jack clothed in a black Little Lord Fauntleroy suit. "But I was born in 1928," Maurice once remarked, "and my father lost every cent he had in the Depression. You only see us in schmattas from then on." The family lived in Brooklyn and scrimped and managed to get by, continually moving from one Bensonhurst neighborhood to another. "Every third year," he explained, "my sister, brother, and I acquired a new apartment, street, and school, because our mother loathed the chaos and stink created by house painters, and in those faraway, dim days, they painted your apartment every third year whether you liked it or not. So my mother got to act out her madness while we would get to see a lot of Brooklyn!"

Throughout his life, Maurice would often regale people with stories about his "cuckoo family," particularly about his mother's immigrant relatives, and he would memorialize them in his picture book *Where the Wild Things Are.* He recounted the genesis of the wild things on innumerable occasions, perhaps most engagingly to Terry Gross in 1986. "I didn't want them to be traditional monsters, like griffins or gorillas," he told her. "I wanted them to be very personal, out of my particular life, and only when they began to appear on my drawing paper did I realize that they were all of my Jewish relatives, my aunts and uncles, who treated me and my brother and sister in such a silly fashion, and they were the real monsters of my childhood.

"They used to come over on Sunday, and we used to get all dressed up and have to sit and listen to their tedious conversation when you'd rather listen to the radio or whatever, and they all said the same dumb things while you were beating time until the food would get put on the table—like, how big you are, how fat you've gotten, you look so good we could eat you up! And because my mother was the slowest cooker in Brooklyn, we knew they *would* have eaten us up. So the only entertainment was watching their bloodshot eyes and noticing how bad their teeth were. You know, children are monstrously cruel about physical defects, and I would examine them closely—the huge noses and the hair curling out of them and the weird moles on the sides of their heads—so I'd glue in on that and later talk about it with my brother and sister. And they became the wild things."

But Maurice's childhood also had a darker side. "I had a very tough time as a kid," he would later disclose. "My parents didn't mean any harm, but they were confused—they didn't speak English, they were living in a foreign country—and they took it out on their kids"; as he told Bill Moyers, "They had problems, emotionally and mentally, and we didn't know that. Because Mommy's supposed to be perfect and should be there *for* you, *love* you, *kiss* you—in every movie we ever saw there was Claudette Colbert hugging her children. We knew that it should be like that, but it wasn't."

Maurice described his mother as being continually anxious, depressed, and withdrawn, but also gruff, abrupt, and rejecting. "I think that any display of feeling embarrassed her," he said, and he reported that when she did try to show her affection, she would do so in bizarre and perplexing ways, rushing into the children's bedroom yelling "Whoooot!" like a banshee and scaring Maurice half to death, or unremittingly tickling his feet, and because he couldn't stand it he'd scream "Why'd you do that?" until she finally stopped. "I'd be angry with her, and she'd be hurt. It was her constant pain not to understand why I didn't realize she was being affectionate.

"I remember when my brother Jack was dying," Maurice told the British journalist Emma Brockes, "he looked at me, and his eyes were all teary, and he said, 'Why were we so unkind to Mama?' And I said, 'Don't do that. We were kids, we didn't understand. We didn't know she was crazy.' When I asked my best friend, Martin, to have lunch at my house and my mother walked through the room, furious—she was always furious—he said, 'Who's that?' And I said, 'We had to hire somebody.' I wouldn't admit it was my mother. And that shame has lasted all my life, that I didn't have the nerve to say, 'That's my mother, that's how she is.'"

Philip Sendak doesn't seem to have played as formative a role in Maurice's childhood as Sadie did, but Maurice was profoundly moved and inspired by the haunting stories that his father would tell his children, improvising, embroidering, and often extending a tale over a period of nights. "One of the most memorable of these," Maurice recalled, "was about a child taking a walk with his father and mother. He becomes separated from them. Snow begins to fall, and the child shivers in the cold. He huddles under a tree, sobbing in terror. An enormous figure hovers over him and says, as he draws the boy up, 'I'm Abraham, your father.' His fear gone, the child looks up and also sees Sarah. He is no longer lost. And when his parents find him, the child is dead. Those stories," Maurice stated, "fused Jewish lore with my father's particular way of shaping memory and desire. That story, for instance, was based on the power of Abraham in Jewish tradition as the father who was always there—a reassuring father even when he was Death."

Maurice frequently contracted illnesses, such as diphtheria, measles, whooping cough, double pneumonia, and scarlet fever. "I was a very sickly child," he explained, "and my parents weren't decorous, they weren't discreet, they didn't know what to say or not to say in front of children, and they always thought I was going to die. So I was aware at a very early age of mortality. It pervaded my soul, and I think it provided me with the basic ingredients of being an artist." Maurice remembered his beloved maternal grandmother sewing him a white suit, dressing him in it along with white stockings and white shoes, then sitting with him on the stoop in front of the house and confiding to him that when the angel of death passed overhead and saw him dressed all in white, he would not be taken, because it would be clear that he was already an angel.

One of Maurice's earliest memories dates from when he was four years old. Convalescing from scarlet fever, he was sitting in the kitchen one day in the lap of his grandmother while his mother baked. "I remember the feeling of pleasant drowsiness," he recalled. "We were in front of a window where she would often sit with her little prayer book and daven and daven and pray, and she pulled the shade up and down like a magic lantern to amuse me. Every time the shade went up, I was thrilled by the sudden reappearance of the backyard, the falling snow, and my brother and sister busy constructing a sooty snowman. Down came the shade—the children had moved, the snowman had grown eyes. I don't remember a single sound."

Recuperating from his illnesses, Maurice would often spend days lying in bed staring out the window, and as he would later remark, "I think it's no accident that windows, or children looking out of windows, or going through windows, would become an obsession in many of my books." In one of his family's Brooklyn apartments there was a window at the foot of his bed that looked out at the backyard with a very boring brick wall. And he remembered a game his father used to play with him. "It wasn't exactly a death game," Maurice said, "but it did move in that direction. My father told me that if I looked out the window and didn't blink and saw an angel, I'd be a very, very lucky child. And so I did that frequently, but I'd always blink, because of course it would hurt not to blink. But I remember that one time I was staring out the window and I didn't blink—my eyes were aching, staring, staring, staring—and I saw it, or imagined I saw it. At first it looked like a dirigible that was passing by, though it wasn't a dirigible, because it went right past my window. But it was a slow-moving angel—she, he, or whatever was moving very gracefully, coming from the left and going across to the right, and not turning to observe me at all. It moved so slowly that I could examine it, and although I don't have a memory of the face, I do have a vivid memory of the hair, the body, and the wings. It took my breath away, and I shrieked and hollered and my father came in, and I said, I *saw* it, and he said that I was a very lucky kid."

As a child, Maurice was very lucky to have had as his own ministering angels a brother and sister who, he stated, "protected me from my parents" and who enabled him to combat and master his own "wild things," all of those emotions that, in his words, "are an ordinary part of children's lives— fear, anger, hate, and frustration—and that children can perceive only as

ABOVE: From *Kenny's Window;* BELOW: From *Higglety Pigglety Pop!*

ungovernable and dangerous forces." As he once confessed, "My rages and my quandaries were severe, and there literally was no one except my brother and sister to work them out with." Natalie was given the task of taking care of him—"My parents were both working hard and didn't have enough time," Maurice explained, "so I was dumped on her"—but it was his brother, Jack, who essentially took on the role of Maurice's protector and savior.

"As a child," he told Emma Brockes, "my brother and I shared a bed. There was no privacy, and we had bedbugs. And to protect me, my brother would say, 'Lie on top of me.' And I would say, 'I'll fall,' and he would reply, 'No you won't, not if you clamp your teeth on my nose.' And I didn't fall to the left, I didn't fall to the right, and the bedbugs didn't get me. They got him. Maybe that's where my love of noses began. He had a great nose." And as he remarked to Terry Gross, "Jack made my childhood bearable, and he saved my life. He drew me away from the lack of comprehension that existed between me and my parents, and he took time with me to draw pictures, read stories, and live a kind of fantastical life. My sister, Natalie, who was nine years older than me, occasionally joined in, but mostly, after all, she was a girl, and all that my parents expected of her was that she should grow up and be very pretty and marry a decent man. I loved her very much, but she didn't have the creative insanity that existed between me and my brother."

"Fantasy," Maurice often declared, "is the best means children have for taming wild things," and Jack provided him with the means to do that. "All I liked to do when I was a kid," he told Leonard Marcus, "was draw—drawing pictures with my brother, putting comics up on the glass window and tracing the characters onto tracing paper or drawing paper and then coloring them. That and making things was all we ever did. We built the entire World's Fair of 1939 in miniature out of wax. The floor of our room was covered with little waxen buildings. Nobody could come in." They also made their own balsa-wood model airplanes and hung them over their beds until they rotted away; and they worked on books together, combining cut-out newspaper photographs and comic strips with sketches of the Sendak family, hand-lettering and drawing pictures on uniform pages, then binding the books with tape and illustrating them with glorious covers.

When Maurice was six years old, he and Jack collaborated on a little book called *They Were Inseparable*—Jack wrote the text and Maurice illustrated it on a shirt cardboard—about a brother and sister who, as Maurice once recounted to me, "had a hankering for each other. We both idolized our sister, Natalie. She was the eldest and by far the prettiest, and we thought she was the crown jewel of the family. So because we idolized her, we made the book about a brother and a sister. They were going to get married, and at the very end of the story an accident occurs. The brother's in the hospital bandaged up like a mummy, they don't think he's going to recover, the sister comes rushing in past doctors and nurses, and they just grab each other—like at the conclusion of *Tosca*—and exclaim, *'We are inseparable!'* Then everybody rushes in to separate them as they jump out the window of Brooklyn Jewish Hospital . . . Yes, you see, we *did* know dimly that there was something wrong, we were punishing them unconsciously."

And he added, "I imagine that all siblings have such feelings, but the learning process makes children become aware that there's a taboo with regard to these feelings, but before you learn that, you do what comes naturally. My parents weren't well-to-do, and we had only two beds—my brother and I slept in one, my sister in the other, and often we'd all sleep in the same bed. My parents would come in—sometimes with my uncle and aunt—and they'd say, 'Look, see how much they like each other, they can't even be separated in bed.' I loved my brother, and I didn't know that that could be this, and this that . . . Kids find that out later. And meanwhile we had a good time."

Natalie, nine-year-old Maurice, and Jack Sendak (1937)

Maurice never visited a museum when he was a child. "People imagine that I was aware of Samuel Palmer and William Blake and English graphics and German fairy tales when I was a kid," he once told me, "but that came later. All I had then were popular influences—comic books, junk books, Gold Diggers movies, monster films, *King Kong, Fantasia*. I remember a Mickey Mouse mask that came on a big box of cornflakes. What a fantastic mask! Such a big, bright, vivid, gorgeous hunk of face! And that's what a kid in Brooklyn knew at the time."

Maurice often proudly pointed out that he and Mickey Mouse were both "born" in 1928, and Mickey was the subject of Maurice's earliest surviving drawing, which dates from 1934, when he was six years old. In an encomium he wrote to his beloved mouse in 1978, he stated, "He was our buddy. My brother and sister and I chewed his gum, brushed our teeth with his toothbrush, played with him in a seemingly endless variety of games, and read about his adventures in comic strips and storybooks. Best of all, our street pal was also a movie star. In the darkened theater, the sudden flash of his brilliant, wild, joyful face—radiating great golden beams—filled me with an intoxicating, unalloyed pleasure." But although love is not love which alters when it alteration finds, Maurice would later bemoan every addition and modification to Mickey's proportions that transformed his soul brother into, as he put it, "a suburbanite, abandoning his street friends and turning into a shapeless, mindless bon vivant."

It was Natalie who gave Maurice his first "official" book, *The Prince and the Pauper*. "A ritual began with that book," he informed the Library of Congress's Virginia Haviland in 1970. "The first thing was to set it up on the table and stare at it for a long time. Not because I was impressed with

Photograph of Maurice Sendak at approximately age five

Mark Twain, but it was just such a beautiful object. Then came the smelling of it . . . it was printed on particularly fine paper, unlike the Disney books I had gotten previous to that. *The Prince and the Paper—Pauper—*smelled good, and it also had a shiny laminated cover. I flipped over that. And it was very solid—I mean, it was bound very tightly. I remember trying to bite into it, which I don't imagine is what my sister intended when she bought the book for me. But the last thing I did with the book was to read it. It was all right. But there's so much more to a book than just the reading: there is a *sensuousness.* I've seen children touch books, fondle books, smell books, and it's all the reason in the world why books should be beautifully produced. And I think that my passion for books and bookmaking started then."

In his early teens, Maurice decided that he wanted to be an illustrator. "I spent hundreds of hours," he recalled, "sitting at my window, sketching neighborhood children at play. I sketched and listened, and those notebooks became the fertile field of my work later on. There is not a book I have written or a picture I have drawn that does not, in some way, owe them its existence." And as he would later tell me, "I was miserable as a kid. I couldn't play stoopball terrific, I couldn't skate great, so I stayed home and drew pictures. You *know* what they all thought of me: sissy Maurie Sendak."

At seventeen he worked after school drawing backgrounds for All-American Comics, adapting Mutt and Jeff strips for comic books, filling in backgrounds (puffs of dust under running heels) and occasionally expanding and embroidering story lines, and he also began illustrating his own books, the first based on the Disney film version of *Peter and the Wolf,* which was soon followed by Oscar Wilde's *The Happy Prince* and Bret Harte's *The Luck of Roaring Camp.*

After graduating from Lafayette High School, Maurice decided not to attend college and instead took a full-time job at Timely Service, a window-display house in lower Manhattan, where he assisted in the construction of store-window models of figures such as Snow White and the Seven Dwarfs made out of chicken wire, papier-mâché, spun glass, plaster, and paint. Inspired by the ingenious wooden mechanisms of Geppetto's workshop in Walt Disney's film *Pinocchio,* Maurice and his brother began to make animated wooden mechanical toys that performed scenes from Hansel and Gretel, Little Miss Muffet, and Old Mother Hubbard, which led to his being hired as a window-display assistant at the world-famous FAO Schwarz toy store in Manhattan.

Maurice's only formal art study took place at this time—two years of evening classes at the Art Students League. Unknown to him, Frances Chrystie, the children's-book buyer at Schwarz, and Richard Nell, the store's display director, arranged for Ursula Nordstrom, the legendary editor in chief of children's books at Harper & Row, to view his work in the Schwarz workrooms, and she immediately asked him to illustrate a translation of Marcel Aymé's *The Wonderful Farm,* a book consisting of seven stories about two little girls' adventures with talking animals on their ensorcelled French farm. It was published in 1951, and it made him, as he proudly noted, an "official person." But he considered *A Hole Is To Dig,* which was published a year later and for which he provided the playful pen-and-ink drawings of rollicking kids that accompanied the poet Ruth Krauss's assemblage of children's definitions, to be "the first book that came together for me."

It has often been noted that the jumping, running, skip-roping, hugging, and altercating children in *A Hole Is To Dig* are all distinctively and unmistakably Sendakian—or perhaps one should say Maurician. "They're all a kind of caricature of me," he once admitted. He noted that people would continually comment on the fact that the children in his books "looked homely, East European Jewish as opposed to the flat, oilcloth look considered normal in children's books," but, as he explained, "they were just Brooklyn kids, old-looking before their time. Many of them resemble the kids I grew up with, and they may well look like little greenhorns just off the boat. They had—some of them, anyway—a kind of bowed look, as if the burdens of the world were on their shoulders." He told Nat Hentoff, "Too many parents and too many writers of children's books don't respect the fact that kids know a great deal and suffer a great deal. My children also show a great deal of pleasure, but often they look defenseless too. Being defenseless is a primary element of childhood. It's not that I don't see the naturalistic beauty of a child. I'm very aware of that beauty, and I could draw it. I know the proportions of a child's body. But I am trying to draw the way children *feel*—or rather, the way I imagine they feel. It's the way I *know* I felt as a child."

Four years after the appearance of *A Hole Is To Dig,* at the age of twenty-seven, Maurice published *Kenny's Window,* which was the first book that he both wrote and illustrated. The early-twentieth-century psychotherapist Alfred Adler once asserted that "the first memory a person recalls will show that individual's fundamental view of life, his first satisfactory crystallization of his attitude, and I would never investigate a personality without asking for the first memory." Perhaps one might apply this notion when discussing a writer's first book.

Kenny's Window, which was published in 1956, tells the story of a little boy who awakens from a dream about a garden above which the moon and the sun are shining simultaneously, side by side, so that "half the garden was filled with yellow morning and the other with dark green night," and in this dream garden he encounters a four-legged rooster that poses seven questions for him to answer (for example, "Can you fix a broken promise?" "What is a very narrow escape?" "Do you always want what you think you want?"). Kenny then sets off on seven journeys in a quest for the answers.

Maurice described the book as "a series of seven fantasies in which Kenny was acting out sometimes irrational rages toward his toy soldiers and then trying to compromise emotionally and get some understanding for those actions, because the assumption was there was no discussing this with his parents. He comes to a resignation, which is, 'I've got to figure it out myself, and I guess I've gotta wait, and I guess I'm going to be alone.'" At the conclusion of the book, however, Kenny, having answered all seven questions, is granted two wishes: one is for a shiny black horse, the other for a ship "with an extra room for a friend."

Maurice himself was less than charitable in his later assessment of this book. "It was the first thing I wrote," he explained to me, "and the pictures are ghastly—I really wasn't up to illustrating my own texts then—and the story itself, to be honest, is nice but overwritten. 'Singing chimes in the city lights and the songs of the city'—today that kind of stuff sounds like Delius combined with Bruckner!" But *Kenny's Window* was in fact an auspicious debut, a work of gentle wisdom that presented in utero some of Maurice's most characteristic themes and obsessions: the child as dreamer, the permeable boundary between real and imaginary worlds, the offstage parents, the belief that adults "don't know how to listen in the night," the parlous journey away from home and the reassuring homecoming, the child's unassuageable rages, the redemptive and transformational powers of fantasy, the protective maternal moon as a child's guardian spirit, and, of course, the window itself, which turns out to be Kenny's correct answer to the rooster's question "What looks inside and what looks outside?"

Kenny was the first of Maurice's intrepid boy heroes, but it was a precocious and vivacious ten-year-old Brooklyn girl who would become his muse. He called her Rosie, and he assiduously observed her playing with her street pals through his parents' second-floor apartment window during the summer

From *Kenny's Window*

and winter of 1948, when he was twenty and temporarily out of a job. He immortalized her in his book *The Sign on Rosie's Door* (1960), as well as, many years later, in both an Off-Broadway musical and a half-hour animated cartoon television special entitled *Really Rosie,* with music composed by Carole King.

Maurice nicknamed his diva "the Fellini of Eighteenth Avenue" and, mesmerized, he observed her dressing up in her mother's and grandmother's clothes and then, as he wrote in his essay "Really Rosie," "imagining herself into being anything she wanted to be, anywhere in or out of the world." Her flamboyant street impersonations were based primarily on the movies— Maurice remembers her managing both Charles Laughton's and Maureen

O'Hara's roles in *The Hunchback of Notre Dame* and lauded it as one of her finest performances. But she also created and enacted roles such as "Alinda the lovely lady singer" or "Alinda the lost girl" ("Who lost you?" her friend, Pudgy, asks her, and she replies, "I lost myself"), forlornly awaiting someone she calls Magic Man, a kind of shtetl Godot, who she hopes will find her and "tell her what to do"—an unimaginable prospect in any case.

"She literally forced her fantasies on her more stolid, less driven friends," Maurice reported, "hoaxing them into pleasure," and he filled almost forty notebooks with Rosie dialogue, Rosie plays, and Rosie original sayings, as well as innumerable sketchbooks in which he depicted her in every conceivable costume, attitude, and pose. "The tremendous energy she put into these dream games probably activated my own creativity," he admitted, and he declared that "she was the living thread, the connecting link between me in my window and the outside over there"—a phrase that would later become the title of one of his books.

Two years after Rosie's spectacular debut, Maurice published the *Nutshell Library* (1962), a boxed set of four miniature volumes—two and a half by four inches in size—which might have pertinently used as its epigraph Hamlet's declaration "O God, I could be bounded in a nutshell and count myself a king of infinite space." This set, which a critic once referred to as a "Compleat Companion to Literacy," included a reptilian alphabet (*Alligators All Around*) in which a carefree alligator family—father (in a bowler hat), mother (in a feathered hat), and son (in a propeller beanie)—gleefully engages in alphabetical activities like "C chasing cats," "O ordering oatmeal," and "R riding reindeers"; a book of months (*Chicken Soup with Rice*), in which an unnamed little boy visits the twelve months of the year, unceasingly revivifying himself with that comforting and restorative elixir of life (in January we see the boy balanced precariously on one skate as he glides obliviously across an icy

ABOVE:

From *The Sign on Rosie's Door*

RIGHT:

"Rosie's Party" from a 1948 Maurice Sendak
sketchbook

In January
it's so nice
while slipping
on the sliding ice
to sip hot chicken soup
with rice.
Sipping once
sipping twice
sipping chicken soup
with rice.

6

From
*Chicken Soup
with Rice
(Nutshell Library)*

pond sipping his fortifying soup out of a bowl); a counting book (*One Was Johnny*), in which ten fierce intruders invade the eponymous hero's little room ("2 was a rat who jumped on the shelf," "6 was a monkey who brought in the mail," "9 was a robber who took an old shoe") until Johnny, having decided that the uninvited guests have outstayed their welcome, threatens to eat them all up unless they scram, which they do, one after the other, counting down from 10 to 1; and, finally, a cautionary tale (*Pierre*), in which a willful and stubborn little boy whose response to every parental request is "I don't care!"

From *Pierre
(Nutshell Library)*

F forever fooling   G getting giggles

From
Alligators All Around
(Nutshell Library)

encounters a famished lion, who looks Pierre right in the eye and asks him if he'd like to die. Needless to say, Pierre doesn't seem to care one way or the other, so the lion ingests him, winds up with a bellyache, and then, since this is a cautionary tale and a teaching moment, regurgitates the lad, who, at least for the nonce, assures his parents that indeed he really *does* care.

9 was a robber who took an old shoe

From
One Was Johnny
(Nutshell Library)

Pierre is one of Maurice's most enduring and popular characters, and Maurice once confided to me that for a long while he had wanted to write something that had the same title as a book by Herman Melville. "But I couldn't call it *Moby-Dick* or *The Confidence Man* or *Typee*," he explained. "It had to be something a little vaguer. Finally I hit on *Pierre*, and then I needed a rhyme for the name, and that's how I came up with Pierre's favorite line, 'I don't care!'" Maurice acknowledged that Pierre was "perhaps the most typical of all my published children," that "he actually could be Rosie playing Pierre," and declared, "A mere change of sex cannot disguise the essential Rosieness of my heroes."

"IT WAS ONLY a short step from Pierre to Max," Maurice once remarked, and with *Where the Wild Things Are* he felt he had come to the end of a long apprenticeship. Later he insisted that all of his previous work could be seen simply as an elaborate preparation for that book. He also insisted that works like *Kenny's Window*, *The Sign on Rosie's Door*, and the *Nutshell Library* should be thought of as "illustrated books," in which pictures are inserted into a text, rather than as "picture books," in which one could observe "an ingenious juxtaposition of picture and word—pictures are left out but the word says it, words are left out but the picture says it," thereby creating a kind of exhilarating rhythmic syncopation and musical counterpoint.

But Maurice would always, and perhaps surprisingly, avow that illustrations should ultimately be servants to the words. Describing his creative modus operandi to his biographer Selma Lanes, he explained, "To me, illustrating means having a passionate affair with the words. I hate to say that it's akin to a mystic rite, but there is no other language to describe what happens.

It is a sensual, deeply important experience. An illustration is an enlargement, an interpretation of the text . . . and you must never illustrate exactly what is written. You must find a space in the text so that pictures can do the work. Then you must let the words take over where words do it best. There's an interchangeability between them, and they each tell two stories at the same time . . . I like to think of myself as setting words to pictures. A true picture book is a visual poem."

Where the Wild Things Are comprises 338 words and ten sentences that shook the world, and they tell the story of Max, a preschooler who, when we first catch sight of him, is dressed in a white wolf suit, looking like an *enfant sauvage* in pajamas, and is careening down the stairs wielding a menacing fork, like Satan with his trident, in ferocious pursuit of his pet dog. His aggravated mother, whom we never see, calls him "WILD THING!" to which Max replies, "I'LL EAT YOU UP!" at which point she banishes him to his room without supper.

When Maurice was young, his mother, Sadie, would occasionally call him *vilder chaiah,* the Yiddish equivalent of "wild thing." And it was perhaps his childhood memory of staring out the window and not blinking and thereby being able to see an angel passing by that served as his inspiration for the famous scene in *Wild Things* where Max confronts and hypnotizes the monsters. "And when he came to the place where the wild things are they roared their terrible roars and gnashed their terrible teeth and rolled their terrible eyes and showed their terrible claws till Max said 'BE STILL!' and tamed them with a magic trick of staring into all their yellow eyes without blinking once and they were frightened and called him the most wild thing of all and made him king of all wild things." It is a scene that the writer and mythologist Joseph Campbell considered to be "one of the greatest moments in literature," and, as Campbell explained to Bill Moyers, "it's only when a man tames his own demons that he becomes king of himself, if not the world." And by not blinking, Max turned his demons into angels.

As of 2013, which was the fiftieth anniversary of the book's publication, *Where the Wild Things Are* had sold more than twenty million copies in thirty-two languages, and in 2015 *Time* magazine named it the number-one best American children's book of all time. But when it was first published, in

till Max said "BE STILL!"
and tamed them with the magic trick

1963, the *Journal of Nursery Education* forewarned parents that "we should not like to have it left about where a sensitive child might find it to pore over in the twilight." Years later, Maurice himself suggested a reason that he thought the book had originally proved to be upsetting to so many people. "Apparently," he told Marcia Alvar, "Max was the first kid in an American children's book to yell at his mother and carry his tantrum past the point where she could endure it. But of course every kid does that, it happens every day all

From *Where the Wild Things Are*

of staring into all their yellow eyes without blinking once
and they were frightened and called him the most wild thing of all

over the world—three times a week at the very least! And every child could identify with something so familiar. So behind the fantasticalness of what's going on with the wild things was an everyday event that the children could all recognize." And, as he would later remark, "When kids perform *Wild Things,* sometimes little girls insist on being Max, and there's nothing wrong with that. Little boys and girls aren't as fixed and tedious and boring as they are with us, they're still young enough to be *both* a little bit and not be upset by it. And Max can easily be a girl—for one thing he's wearing a unisex suit—and a little girl can of course go through exactly the same experience that he went through . . . and so maybe she could be called Maxine or Max-ette!"

But whatever his or her name, it is specifically the three fantastical, wordless, full-color, double-page spreads, breaking out of confining borders and depicting the bacchanalian "wild rumpus"—what have been called "the best-thumbed pages in contemporary children's literature"—that have enraptured and continue to enrapture millions of children throughout the world. One of the most gratifying moments in Maurice's life occurred when he was told about a severely autistic child who, after looking intently at those rumpus illustrations, clutched the book to his chest and spoke for the very first time.

SEVEN YEARS AFTER the publication of *Wild Things,* Maurice would return to his indelible childhood obsession with his old buddy Mickey Mouse, explaining that it seemed "natural and honest to reach out openly to that early best friend, while eagerly exploring a very private favorite childhood fantasy." That fantasy turned out to be *In the Night Kitchen,* one of his most inventive, dazzling, and controversial works. Published in 1970, the book is Maurice's joyous homage to Laurel and Hardy comedies; Busby

Berkeley musicals; *King Kong;* the cheap full-color picture books and comic books of the 1930s; the newspaper cartoon strip *Little Nemo in Slumberland* by the turn-of-the-century funny-papers fantasist Winsor McCay, about a boy who dreamed himself into fabulous adventures from which he awoke in the last frame; and, of course, Mickey himself, whose name Maurice gave to the little hero of his new book.

We first see Mickey asleep in his bed, awakened by "a racket in the night" ("thump, dump, clump, bump") that is coming either from his parents' adjoining bedroom or from something he thinks he hears downstairs. Enraged, he shouts out, "Quiet down there!" and suddenly finds himself floating out of his bed and out of his pajamas and falling into a surrealistic

Seven panels from *Little Nemo in Slumberland* by Winsor McCay (1906)

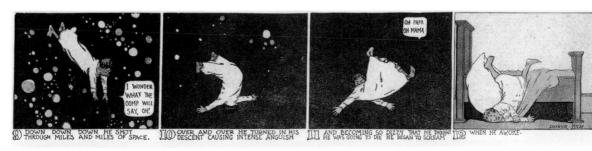

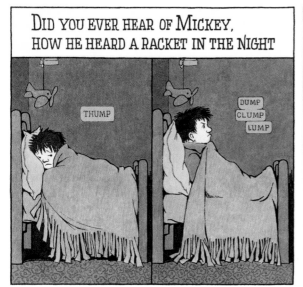

From *In the Night Kitchen*

underworld kitchen where he lands, naked, in the middle of an enormous bowl of dough. A trio of grinning bakers who look like Oliver Hardy, adorned with brush mustaches and carrying a sack of flour, a box of baking soda, and a container of salt, begin to mix the now-submerged Mickey into batter, then take the bowl and are about to place it into a Mickey-Oven to bake a delicious Mickey-Cake when, just in the nick of time, Mickey pops out and exclaims, "I'm not the milk and the milk's not me! I'm Mickey!" Kneading, punching, and pounding the dough until it becomes a Hop Harrigan plane, he puts a blue measuring-cup helmet on his head and soars into the moonlit night, flying over the top of the Milky Way in search of milk for the bakers' cake, and lands his plane on a giant glass milk bottle, into which he dives, singing, "I'm in the milk and the milk's in me. God bless milk and God bless me!" Scooping some milk into his helmet, he pours it into the grateful bakers' batter bowl down below, and as they joyfully mix, beat, and bake the batter, we observe a triumphant Mickey standing on the top of the bottle, crying out "Cock-a-doodle doo!" and then watch him sliding down the side of the bottle back into his own bed and into his pajamas, carefree and dry. "And thanks to Mickey," the book concludes, "we have cake every morning."

"When *In the Night Kitchen* was first published," Maurice recalled, "I was told that you can't have a penis in a book for children because it might frighten them. Yet parents take their children to museums where they see Roman statues with their dicks broken off. You'd think that would frighten them more. But 'art' is somehow desexualized in people's minds. My God, that would make the great artists vomit. I once heard that in a nursery school courtyard in Switzerland there was a statue of a nude boy running. It was anatomically correct except for the genitals, which were a bronze blur. The children were upset by this, and their parents complained, and the boy's genitals were then carved in. In this country it would be the other way round—we prefer the blur, the fig leaf, the diaper."

But almost everyone has acknowledged that *In the Night Kitchen* is a graphic masterpiece. Using a felt-tip pen, Maurice made broadly outlined, comic book–style drawings with flat, bold, and sharply contrasting colors to create an astonishing surreal nighttime Manhattan skyline made up of buildings that are actually cream cartons, coffee tins, jam and baking soda jars, sacks of shortening, saltshakers, bottles of baby syrup and orange–flower water, and kitchen utensils like nutcrackers, egg beaters, whisks, and bottle openers. And looming over them is the giant glass milk-bottle skyscraper that Maurice envisioned as the Empire State Building.

From *In the Night Kitchen*

In this City of the Night Kitchen he also included many private references and associations. A bottle labeled KNEITEL'S FANDANGO refers to a dealer in Mickey Mouse memorabilia named Kenny Kneitel. On a cream carton are inscribed the addresses of two of the Brooklyn apartment buildings where Maurice lived as a child, 1717 WEST 6TH ST. and 1756 58th ST.; and on the façade of a coconut box is written PATENTED JUNE 10TH 1928, which was Maurice's birthday. Most significantly, a container of tomato paste is labeled SADIE'S BEST, and on another container are written the words PHILIP'S BEST TOMATOES. (Maurice dedicated *Night Kitchen* to his parents.)

There is also a carton simply labeled EUGENE'S. In *Kenny's Window,* the four-legged rooster grants Kenny two wishes, and Kenny asks for a shiny black horse and "an extra room for a friend." For Maurice, that friend would turn out to be Eugene Glynn, who would be his partner for fifty years. A psychiatrist and art critic, Glynn, who died in 2007, worked in public medicine, specializing in the treatment of adolescents, and was the author of insightful writings on both art and psychoanalysis that were posthumously published in *Desperate Necessity,* a collection of essays for the cover of which Maurice painted Eugene's portrait.

Maurice once confessed, "All I wanted was to be straight so my parents could be happy. They never, never, never knew." It was only when he was eighty that he publicly outed himself, and he did so in a 2008 interview he gave to Patricia Cohen in *The New York Times.* At the end of the interview, Cohen asked Maurice if there was anything he had never been asked. He paused for a few moments, and then responded that no one had ever asked him if he was gay, and he said that he was, adding that he hadn't previously felt that it was anybody's business, and had moreover been wary of doing so because of his concern that the idea of a gay man writing children's books might have hurt his career when he was in his twenties and thirties, and even when he was creating controversial picture books such as *Where the Wild Things Are* and *In the Night Kitchen.*

Night Kitchen had a fascinating genesis. "When I was a child," Maurice informed Virginia Haviland, "there was an advertisement which I remember very clearly. It was for the Sunshine Bakers, and the advertisement read 'We Bake While You Sleep!' It seemed to me the most sadistic thing in the world, because all I wanted to do was stay up and watch. And it seemed so absurdly cruel and arbitrary for them to do it while I slept, and also for them to think I would think that was terrific stuff on their part, you know, and would eat their produce on top of that. It bothered me a good deal, and I remember I used to save the coupons showing the three fat little Sunshine Bakers going off to this magic place, wherever it was, at night to have their fun, while I had to go to bed. So this book was a sort of vendetta book to get back at them and to say that I am now old enough to stay up at night and know what is happening in the Night Kitchen!"

But Maurice did, in fact, know exactly where the Sunshine Bakers engaged in their nighttime work, and he actually visited "this magic place" in 1939, when he was eleven years old. It was the year of the World's Fair, which he desperately wanted to go to, so he entreated his twenty-year-old sister, Natalie, to take him. His parents were always working, so Natalie, in Maurice's words, "had to schlep me everywhere," and she hated doing so because she had a new boyfriend, but she was able to talk him into taking her brother along with them. "And when we got there," as Maurice recounted the story in an interview for the Rosenbach Museum and Library, "she planted me in front of the Sunshine Bakery, and this aroma came out of this white building—it was the smell of biscuits and cake and flour and milk, and it was better than sex, better than anything in the whole world, and I just stood there sniffing. And then these little fat bakers with mustaches came out and stood on the balcony and they waved, and I stood downstairs and waved back to them—I don't know how long we waved at each other—but when I turned around, my sister and her boyfriend were gone. They'd *dumped* me! But that scene at the bakery was emblematic and it became the emblem for *Night Kitchen*—the bakers, the lusciousness of cooking, of kneading with your hands, of undressing and floating in this sensuosity of milk . . . and thus driving every librarian crazy! I really love that book, much more than *Wild Things,* because it's really a gut book with a profound love for luscious things."

But Maurice's boyhood fantasy of New York City as "the most magical of all lands, rarely visited but much dreamed of," was another important childhood memory that played an equally important role in the gestation of

Postcard of the Sunshine Bakers' Exhibit at the 1939 New York World's Fair

From *In the Night Kitchen*

Night Kitchen. "I lived in Brooklyn," he explained, "and to travel to Manhattan was a big deal, even though it was so close. I couldn't go by myself, so my sister would occasionally take my brother and me to Radio City Music Hall, or the Roxy, or some such place. Now, the point of going to New York was that you *ate* in New York. Somehow New York represented eating, and eating in a very fashionable, elegant, superlatively mysterious place like Longchamps. You got dressed up, and you went uptown, and it was night when you got there, and there were lots of windows blinking, and you went straight to a place to eat. It was one of the most exciting things of my childhood. Cross the bridge, and see the city approaching, and get there, and have your dinner, and then go to a movie, and come home. So *In the Night Kitchen* is a kind of homage to New York City, the city I loved so much, and still love."

Part Two

Maurice was a city boy who lived in and loved Manhattan for most of his adult life, but he also for a long time dreamed of living in the country, and although he kept an apartment in the city, he decided in 1972 to buy a house six miles north of Ridgefield, Connecticut. I was supposed to visit him on June 10, 1976, in order to interview him for a profile I was going to write for *Rolling Stone* magazine, but early that morning I received a call from him. Visit postponed, I thought.

"My dogs aren't well," he said sadly, "but I think it will cheer me up to have company . . . It's my birthday today."

"Happy birthday!" I exclaimed. "What would you like as a present?"

"Well, if it's no trouble, a sandwich from a deli. Any kind. Anything. It's hopeless around here."

"What about hot pastrami with coleslaw and mustard on rye?" I suggested.

"Fantastic."

"And pickles?"

"Fantastic. And perhaps a really gooey chocolate layer cake for dessert?"

WHEN MAURICE PICKED me up at the train station, he apologized for being late. "There are hundreds of children parading through town," he said incredulously. As we began to drive slowly back to his house, I saw hordes of kids marching silently along the roads, as if they were following an invisible and inaudible Pied Piper.

"What's going on?" I wondered aloud.

"I live here," he replied bemusedly.

Ridgefield is a small town which, coincidentally, was the birthplace of Samuel Griswold Goodrich (1793–1860), perhaps the most influential figure in nineteenth-century American children's literature, whose more than one hundred Peter Parley books sold seven million copies in this country. Illustrated with wood engravings, they were generally nationalistic but occasionally tolerant utilitarian schoolbooks written in the compendious and moronic style that served as the model for generations of first-grade primers: "Here I am! My name is Peter Parley! I am an old man. I am very gray and lame. But I have seen a great many things, and had a great many adventures, and I love to talk about them . . . And do you know that the very place where Boston stands was once covered with woods, and that in these woods lived many Indians? Did you ever see an Indian? Here is a picture of some Indians."

Aside from the fact that, a century apart, two creators of children's literature lived just a few miles down the road from each other, writers more dissimilar than Goodrich and Sendak would be hard to imagine. Goodrich particularly objected to the moral obliquity of *Puss in Boots* and *Jack the Giant Killer* ("tales of horror, commonly put into the hands of youth, as if for the express purpose of reconciling them to vice and crime") and detested nursery rhymes, declaring that even a child could make them up. To prove his point, he produced the following nonsense on the spot: "Higglety, pigglety, pop! / The dog has eaten the mop; / The pig's in a hurry, / The cat's in a flurry, / Higglety, pigglety, pop!"

Irony upon irony. A century later, Maurice wrote and illustrated one of his most mysterious and haunting works, *Higglety Pigglety Pop! or There Must Be More to Life* (1967), a modern fairy tale about a dog named Jennie—modeled after Maurice's beloved Sealyham terrier—who, although she has two windows through which to view the outside world, as well as two comfortable pillows, two bowls to eat from, and a devoted master, decides one day to pack her leather bag and leave home in order to search for "something more than everything." She eventually makes her debut as the leading lady of a World Mother Goose Theater production of the Samuel Goodrich nursery rhyme with her costars Miss Rhoda, Pig, Cat, and a lion reminiscent of the one in *Pierre,* who has a taste for nurses and babies. At the end of the book, Jennie heartbreakingly writes home to her master: "As you probably noticed, I went away forever. I am very experienced now and very famous. I am even a star. Every day I eat a mop, twice on Saturday. It is made of salami and that is my favorite. I get plenty to drink too, so don't worry. I can't tell you how to get to the Castle Yonder because I don't know where it is. But if you ever

From *Higglety Pigglety Pop!*

Maurice Sendak and his dog,
Jennie, in the 1950s.
Photo by Vito Fiorenza

come this way, look for me." (The real Jennie died almost one month before the publication of *Higglety Pigglety Pop!*)

There were two great muses in Maurice's creative life, Rosie and Jennie, both of them aspiring actresses. Jennie made innumerable appearances in his books—we catch sight of her napping under the bed in *Kenny's Window,* sitting on a bench outside one of the Brooklyn apartment buildings in *The Sign on Rosie's Door,* running away from a menacing, fork-wielding Max in *Where the Wild Things Are,* and her name is inscribed on the flour sack of one of the *Night Kitchen* bakers. Maurice immortalized both Rosie and Jennie, and his Brooklyn diva bedazzled him, but it was the latter whom he declared to be "the love of my life."

WHEN WE ARRIVED at Maurice's sprawling white clapboard house, which was surrounded by beautiful ash, sugar maple, dogwood, and locust trees—

"my goyishe Franchot Tone house," he used to call it—we were vociferously greeted by the three dogs that lived with him: Agamemnon, a male shepherd; Erda, a female shepherd; and Io, a female golden retriever. "Zeus had a fling with Io," Maurice informed me, "and jealous Hera transformed her into a bull calf who was bitten by a gadfly throughout eternity. The minute I saw Io, she looked like a victim—blond and beautiful." And upon entering the house, I found myself in a wondrous brave new world. On one of the walls was a glorious Winsor McCay triptych showing Little Nemo and a princess walking down a resplendent garden path surrounded by daffodils with smiling faces, and stunning posters by Edward Penfield, Will Bradley, Toulouse-Lautrec, and Pierre Bonnard.

Maurice Sendak in his studio (1976).
Photo © Nancy Crampton

Maurice led me into his womblike studio, located at the end of a corridor just off the kitchen, and I noticed, among other things, a cabinet of vintage Mickey Mouse toys; a pillow in the shape of the *Night Kitchen*'s Mickey and his bottle of milk; a contingent of stuffed wild things from admirers around the world; a portrait of young Mozart at the pianoforte; original drawings by Beatrix Potter (Maurice would eventually purchase her walking sticks) and Jean de Brunhoff, the author of Maurice's much-beloved Babar books; and above the desk a honeymoon photograph of Philip and Sadie Sendak.

Maurice then showed me some of his other rooms, where shelves were filled with rare books, many of them first and signed editions by Herman Melville, Charles Dickens, Henry James, and Beatrix Potter. (Several years later he obtained Melville's traveling writing desk, as well as his contract for the novel *Pierre* with Harper and Brothers Publishers.) When we returned to the dining room, the table was piled high with presents from some of Maurice's friends: a Mickey Mouse mirror and a Mickey Mouse music box, an eighteenth-century tin coach from Germany, miniature bottles of Dry Sack, a floral bouquet. As my celebratory offering, I placed the sandwiches that I'd brought from the city on the table.

"You told me on the phone that you were starting to write the text for your new book," I said to Maurice as we sat down to have lunch, "but you mentioned that you were a bit stymied at the moment."

"This will be the last part of my trilogy that includes *Where the Wild Things Are* and *In the Night Kitchen*," he informed me, "and of the three books, this one will be the strangest. It's so dense already, and I don't know what it means, and I can't get beyond the first seven lines. But I'll get there, I'll finish it, and it will be terrific, and it will turn a lot of people off, more than they've been turned off before, I think. But it's going to be so rich.

"I feel it in me," he continued, "like a woman having a baby, all that life churning on inside me. Unconsciously, it moves, stretches, yawns . . . it's get-ting ready to get born. It knows exactly what it is, only I don't know with my conscious mind what it is, but every day I get a little clue. My unconscious says, Maurice, listen, dum-dum, here's a word for you, see what you can make of it. And it throws it out, and I catch it: Oh, a word! Fantastic! Terrific! And then I do without for three days, and my unconscious says, Shit, this guy is too much to believe! He walks, he drinks, he sits, he'll do anything to stop being an artist. Throw him another word, otherwise he'll sit there forever and have a coronary. And one by one it throws me words."

"Is it happening at the right time now?" I asked him.

"Is it the right time for a book!" he exclaimed. "It's like getting preg-nant when you've just gone crazy and you've found out that you have cancer and that your house has burned down. Emotionally, I'm in turmoil. I didn't want to get pregnant now. When I write the book, it may be an abortion, but let's hope not. I'm definitely with life, as they say, sitting like a mother on a stump, thinking, Thank you, God, thank you."

"D. H. Lawrence," I interjected, "used to describe the pregnant mother as feeling at one with the world."

"The *maven* on how women feel!" Maurice retorted. "What does that mean? It's so tacky, it sounds like being glued to something. I don't feel at one with the world, I never have and I never will. The only thing that's miraculous is the creative act, and I call it miraculous because I don't under-stand it. I don't understand, for example, how Mozart could write semi-trivial but deliciously funny and cute letters to Daddy at the very moment he was composing his sublime works. And when Daddy says, 'Look, Wolfgang, I don't want you messing around in Munich, you're there to get a job, I don't like your going dancing every night—your mother's written to me all about it. Pull yourself together. You're not the type to do this kind of thing. Your loving father,' Mozart would write back, 'But Daddy, Daddy, I just went out with Fräulein So-and-so, she's a nice girl, I had two dances, came home at eleven o'clock, I've been good, haven't been drinking wine, and on top of that I just wrote the horn concerto, two violin concertos, and the famous Sinfonia Concertante. Isn't that enough for this week, Daddy? I'll try and be better.'

"Now, of course I made that up, but that's the sound of it, and Mozart composed those pieces that same week he was thinking those nothing thoughts and trying to get his boring father off his back. *That* I don't understand, *that* is a mystery to me, and I'm sure it was a mystery to him. The fact that he could sit down with incredible gurgling versatility and pour forth. Where did it come from? It was simply there."

"I've often read that you deeply love Mozart's music," I said, "and I'm reminded that when an interviewer once asked Rossini who the greatest composer was, he replied, 'Beethoven.' And when the interviewer then said to him, 'What about Mozart?' Rossini replied, 'Mozart is not the greatest composer, he is the *only* composer!'"

Maurice smiled. "Mozart is one of my gods. I'm in love with Mozart's music, and I should tell you that *Outside Over There* is in fact going to be an homage to him."

"When you read Mozart's letters," I said, "you sometimes get the impression that he was a bit like a child."

"Yes, from what we know he was overwhelmed by Daddy, he was constantly placating him, and while he was doing that he was creating something that was completely beyond his father, beyond anyone's father, and beyond any of us two hundred years later. *That's* the miracle. I've read a dozen books about him, but best of all are his letters. I'm reading them now and every one of them is beautiful, no matter how trivial it is. And they're very scatological—

not only Wolfgang's but sober Frau Mozart's as well. 'When you go to bed, shit well till it busts,' she writes to her husband. Now, you *know* she's not a maniac. And Wolfgang writes something like 'My darling, my quintessential sister, I kiss you, stuff your arse in your mouth tonight and bite with all your heart. Then shit and let it bust good.' It's so strange! What does it mean? Very conceivably one might think that Mozart was an anal retentive, that he never got past the toilet-training stage. But it was the eighteenth century, and there's also that very Germanic quality of every day being based on the quality of the bowel movement."

"I seem to remember," I added, "that in one of his letters he writes: 'Do we live to shit, or shit to live?' That's very advanced existential humor!"

"It's that combination of gravity and grace that I love so much in Mozart," Maurice declared. "He's the ideal, and God knows I'm not like him. I'm more like Beethoven. And recently I also began reading about him and his relationship with his nephew, Karl. To me, Beethoven exemplifies the grandiosity of the artist who can sit down and then out of *nothing* make something, just pulling it out of the air, which gives you a very inflated sense of your own worth. But when Karl wanted to go out, Beethoven suffered terribly. The dummy couldn't force a little boy to love him the way he could force the Hammerklavier sonata to appear on paper. *That* was absolute magic, but here the magic didn't apply. The endless convulsions he went through and the endless sensitivity and vulnerability and jealousies. If Beethoven looked out the window and saw his nephew walk down the street and smile at a neighbor, Beethoven would double over in pain: 'Karl smiled at that neighbor, but he never smiled at me that way! Why must I suffer the indifference of this little fucking child!' "

"It sounds as if he were the boy's mother," I observed.

"Yes," Maurice agreed, "he became the mother to this child."

"And he also sounds like a kind of Pygmalion."

"But he's not trying to *create* this creature," Maurice said, "he's trying to *force* the creature. He's taken the child and is making believe that it's other than what it really is. The child probably did love him, but Beethoven's special kind of love—I-hypnotize-you-into-total-love—overlooked what genuinely did come from the child: affection, pleasure in having an extraordinary man named Beethoven as his uncle. But it wasn't enough for him."

"Do you sometimes feel that way?" I asked Maurice.

"Yes, I do identify with Beethoven—it's like the Achilles' heel of the artist who lives on a grandiose plane, conjuring up his art, but failing in real life because his inflated ego can't be satisfied. In my own life I clench my teeth with rage when it doesn't work my way, because my big inflated ego isn't satisfied, and I don't know how to switch it on and off. You think you're working on something fantastic, and then you turn to real life—say, your dog—and you say to her, Come here, darling, and she walks past you and lets someone else pet her. That's what it's like. I don't like Beethoven the man, but I have tremendous sympathy for him . . . I hope"—Maurice suddenly grimaced—"that you don't think of me as some kind of schlub."

"You seem to have both Mozart and Beethoven in you," I suggested diplomatically.

"But more Beethoven," Maurice admitted. "Mozart is the ideal, but I'm not good-humored, I don't deal with the problems of life very well, and that's probably why I dislike Beethoven so much. The rages, the temper, the irrationality . . ."

"It sounds a little bit like Max, if you don't mind my saying so," I interjected.

"Yes," Maurice agreed, "it's the heated, feverish carrying-on that I hate so much, without any of the cool pleasure of Mozart."

"Speaking of pleasure," I said, "I can't help but think of Mickey in *Night Kitchen,* who really does live out his dream of pleasure, doesn't he?"

Maurice nodded. "When Mickey is swimming in the milk and floating naked, every part of his body having a sensuous experience, it's just remembering the deepest kind of pleasure that we all once had. It was all paradise, we all once lived in the Garden of Eden, and as we grew up we no longer did. That's what growing up is all about—we have to grow up—but that doesn't mean we must or should forget what that minute of pleasure was all about. Some people objected to Mickey having this sensuous experience, as if that's naughty. Why? Why are we so screwed up, including me? But at least creatively I try to convey the memory of a time in life when it was a pleasure."

"I've also noticed that a lot of your characters, both human and animal, seem to get a lot of pleasure from eating or threatening to eat each other up," I mentioned. "In *Pierre,* the lion eats Pierre. In *Higglety Pigglety Pop!* Jennie eats a mop. And then, of course, Max threatens to eat up his mother, and Kenny expresses a desire to eat up his teddy bear, Bucky. People and things get swallowed and are then regurgitated. What's this all about?"

"Well, I'm certainly not going to disgorge this hot pastrami sandwich that you were nice enough to bring me—it's delicious, and I feel better already," he said, laughing. "But you know, I used to love *biting* into my books when I was a child, so maybe it's a hang-up from that time . . . but a pleasant one: things being eaten and then given out again—it's an image that constantly appeals to me, and to most children too. It's such a primary fantasy of childhood—the pleasure of putting things in the mouth, of chewing, of swallowing, of shitting and pissing. Before children are told it's not a nice thing—the whole toilet-training process—there's nothing nicer."

"But sometimes things get a little scarier than usual," I observed. "I can

Fantasy sketch by Maurice Sendak

never forget an astonishing fantasy sketch you did that shows a child devouring his mother, and in this case, Mama doesn't get disgorged."

"Yes," Maurice admitted, "some people were shocked by that. But of course children must feel that the big luminous breast hanging over their head is sent there by God. Obviously it's there for you, why not? Until you're told differently, how are you going to know? There's something both monstrous and poignant about it: the poignancy comes from the fact that a child's going to realize soon enough that it's not so, that he'll have to compete for it, but that for the second's worth that it's there it's a glorious pleasure. And all I'm saying is, what's wrong with the pleasure? Why must we assume that the knowing is the correct thing and that the pleasure is the bad thing, which is what most people feel?"

"Well," I interjected, "someone could look at it another way: mother destroys child, child destroys mother."

"But I don't understand the destructive aspect," Maurice disagreed. "In my little cartoon, the baby eats the mother—on the surface what could be more destructive? But in fact the child doesn't think of it as a destructive act, it's the most natural thing to him: if you have that much of the mother, have more!

"Incidentally," he added, "I did another and earlier version of this sketch in the 1950s, and in that version the baby comes out of a fish that's swallowed him. The mother is there, furious that that baby's been lost—turns the baby over on her knee and spanks him. And he, in his rage, this tiny baby in his little diaper, pulls away from her, pulls out a gun, and shoots her dead. *That* sketch, shall we say, was *unsynthesized*. The earlier version was done while my mother was living, and the later one after she died. So obviously I thought and rethought a lot about her during that interval."

"I remember the flap you caused with naked Mickey," I said to Maurice. "But take a look at these illustrations I brought up to show you from Jacques Stella's seventeenth-century *Games & Pastimes of Childhood*—all of them depicting naked little putti capering and frolicking."

"It's an amazing coincidence," he said excitedly. "I was given this book again recently because *Outside Over There* is in part concerned with babies doing odd things, and I've been looking at it for weeks. The illustrations are beautiful . . . and strange. There's a hallucinatory quality about them: on the surface they're just children playing games, but why are they all naked? And they're all moving with the agility of adults—babies can't play like that. Yet we often make a mistake of reading heavy and tedious psychological overtones into things that in the seventeenth and eighteenth centuries weren't considered that way at all. We overload and overcharge meaning because we're twentieth-century people. And maybe we should, but it's not necessarily so. At that time, that book was just another book, nothing special. Putti were all over the churches, all over sculptures and architecture—naked

"Toy Cannons" from *Games & Pastimes of Childhood* by Jacques Stella (1657)

children were a favorite art form. But I couldn't do that book today, I'd be thrown out of the country. But *that* book is a classic."

"In Randall Jarrell's *Fly by Night*," I reminded him, "you did extraordinary drawings of an eight-year-old boy flying naked in his dream."

"I tried to draw the boy first with pajamas," Maurice explained. "But he looked too much like an ad for Fruit of the Loom. Then I tried him wrapped in sheets and blankets, but it looked too baroque. He had to be naked. But I know they're going to say it's typically me, arbitrarily making somebody nude. I had a picture showing a girl with her vagina in full view in a drawing for George MacDonald's *The Light Princess,* and nobody made a fuss about that, which makes me think the whole world is male chauvinist—vaginas don't count. And *Outside Over There* will have another naked child, and God knows what she'll be doing!"

"What's *Fly by Night* about?" I asked him.

"It's a dream: the boy David dreams. Every night he dreams he floats. During the daytime he tries to remember that he can float at night, but he can't. When he wakes up he can't remember. And the entire story is about what happens to him in this one dream. He floats out of his house, over certain animals, and each of them has a little poem, written by Jarrell—they're delicious poems, and yet they're much deeper, with a kind of funny, starved feeling in them.

"David meets the owl, floats into her nest, and she sings David and her baby a song about getting a little sister and being taken care of by a mother. For me, that's what the whole book is about, although it may not have been for Randall. It's about being starved for a mother or for safety or protection or for some place where you can nest or land or be. But it has a happy ending. David comes home, slides back into his bed, and when he wakes up, there's his mother, who's made him breakfast."

"Just like Max's mother has made him supper!" I said.

"Exactly. And David looks at his mother, she looks familiar—someone looks just like her. Of course it's the owl—he's losing all memory of his dream. And you know, I drew myself as a baby in the book—you can see me in my mother's arms in the book's only double-spread picture. I may have taken a very lopsided and fanciful view of the story, but what I read into it was a great hunger pain—that longing I once felt in Jarrell's *The Animal Family*—and I interpreted it as being a looking-for-Mama pain . . . Maybe it's my pain."

"You mentioned that your new book is going to be about babies."

"It is, and in fact most of my books are about babies, and it seems as

From *Fly by Night*

if I've been doing the same thing since I was six years old. I'm a few inches taller and I have a graying beard, but otherwise there's not much different. I love babies' faces and I draw them all the time. They're uncanny. When my father was dying, he'd dwindled—he had the body shape of a boy—and as I held him, I noticed that his head had become bigger than the rest of him and was rolling back like an infant's. It was like protecting a baby. Death at that moment was like going to sleep: 'Shhh, it will be all right.' It's what you'd say to a feverish baby, except that he was dead.

"Infants' heads are wonderful to draw," he continued, "because they're so big and ungainly. You know how they fall back? Babies cry when they're held badly because they know they can be dropped. And when some klutz picks them up, they scream, and he'll say, 'I don't know why the baby's cry-ing,' and then he hands it back to Mama and suddenly it's all right because baby knows when it's safe. They're enormous kvetches with those mean little faces—'Give me this!'—and at the same time there's a look that they get that makes them so vulnerable, poignant, and lovable."

"There's a theme that appears in much of your work," I observed, "and I can only hint at because it's difficult to formulate or describe. But it has something to do with lines like 'As I went over the water, / The water went over me,' from your illustrated nursery rhyme book *As I Went Over the Water,* or Mickey's 'I'm in the milk and the milk's in me' from *Night Kitchen.*"

"Obviously I have one theme," Maurice said, "and it's also going to be in *Outside Over There.* It's not that I have such original ideas, just that I'm good at doing variations on the same idea over and over again. You can't imagine how relieved I was to find out that Henry James admitted he had only a couple of themes and that all of his books were based on them. That's all we need as artists—one power-driven fantasy or obsession, then to be clever enough to do variations, like a series of variations by Mozart. My new book is *Wild Things* again, it's *Night Kitchen* again, it's *Higglety Pigglety Pop!* again. The same things draw me, the same images."

"What is this one obsession?" I asked him.

"I'm not about to tell you—not because it's a secret, but because I can't verbalize it."

"There's a line by Bob Dylan in his song 'Just Like a Woman' that talks about being 'inside the rain.'"

"Inside the rain?"

"When it's raining outside," I explained, "I often feel inside myself, as if I were inside the rain . . . as if the rain were my *self*. That's the sense I get from Dylan's image and from your books as well. Being outside and inside at one and the same time."

"It's strange you say that," said Maurice, "because rain has become one of the most potent images in *Outside Over There*. It sort of scares me that you mentioned that line. Maybe that's what rain means. It's such an important ingredient in my new book, and I've never understood what it meant. There was a thing about me and the rain when I was a child: if I could summon it up in one sentence, I'd be happy to. It's such connected tissue. But I don't want to say too much about my book yet—it's waiting to be born."

Part Three

This is the way the book begins:

Papa is away at sea, and Mama is standing in a cove on the edge of a craggy, rock-strewn shore, looking out toward four distant full-rigged sailing ships in the gold-flecked, sunset-reflecting waters. In this eighteenth-century Northern Romantic landscape with its gnarled tree, jagged peaks, and snagged rock faces under a luminous, silken sky, Mama is wearing a capacious, full-length, russet-red dress and a mauve-gray leghorn bonnet and scarf. Beside her, also looking out to sea, is her nine-year-old daughter, Ida, in a Marian-blue dress;

her incongruously outsized bare feet, with their thick anklebones and tough Achilles tendons, are placed solidly on a small flat boulder. In her arms she is carrying her one-year-old baby sister, whose head is as large as Ida's and who wears a floppy yellow cap with an orange sash that is billowing out in the wind. Her face is turned toward us, but her eyes seem to be focused on something far away. And at the other side of the cove, like unacknowledged shadows at the edge of consciousness, are two baleful, faceless goblins in mauve-gray hooded robes, sitting in a rowboat with a wooden ladder at its side.

The family returns to their arbor, where we see Mama seated on a bench in a shaded latticework bower entwined with vines, staring off into the distance as if narcotized, oblivious of Ida, who stands behind her with the bawling baby in her arms; and in the middle of the arbor an equally entranced German shepherd is lying on the grass in a world of its own. Disconnected from each other, they all seem to be in the thrall of an unidentified contagion, but on the far side of the arbor the two faceless goblins with their ladder are on the move.

With Mama immobilized, Ida must tend to her sister on her own, so she carries the crying baby into the parlor, where, on the wall, a framed portrait of their papa is reflected in a mirror, and places her into a crib, then picks up her magic yellow wonder horn and turns her back on her sister to play a calming melody. But during this moment of distraction, the goblins climb into the room on their ladder through an open window and snatch the baby, leaving a ghost-white, bug-eyed changeling made of ice in her stead. Placing her wonder horn on the floor, Ida turns around, lifts the ice baby from the crib, and while hugging it and murmuring, "How I love you," she watches in shock as it melts slowly in her arms, until all that remains are two icy hands and her sister's floppy yellow cap floating in a puddle on the floor.

Like one of the ancient Greek Furies, Ida, with arms raised and fists clenched, declaims, "They stole my sister away to be a nasty goblin's bride!" And taking on the role of an avenging woman warrior, she prepares to reclaim her sister. The window of the room expands, and as if to mirror Ida's enraged emotional state, pullulating sunflowers burst in, the sky ominously darkens, the waves rise, lightning strikes, and outside we see a square-rigger foundering in a tempest. But as the storm subsides, Ida dons her mother's voluminous golden-yellow rain cloak with its voluptuous pleats and folds, tucks her wonder horn in a pocket, climbs out her window, and begins to float into outside over there.

But Ida has climbed out the window backward and upside down, and now unable to search for, confront, and rescue her sister from the faceless goblins, she floats aimlessly on her back on a bank of dark cumulus clouds through a hallucinatory moonlit dreamscape, while unseen below her is a mysterious oil lamp with its golden flame; a baby sitting alone in an underground cave, guarded by two goblins; two sailors resting on a boulder alongside their boat; a shepherd with his crook, asleep beside his sheep; and, far down below in the chthonian depths, Ida's spellbound mama, sitting with her eyes closed in her bower, as if she were dreaming this entire visionary scene.

And then from off in the sea, like a voice out of the whirlwind, Ida hears her papa singing: "If Ida backwards in the rain / would only turn around again / and catch these goblins with a tune / she'd spoil their kidnap honeymoon!" Tumbling right side around, she travels head-on into an underground grotto, where she discovers five shape-shifting goblins who have turned into five naked, crying babies, just like her sister. Removing her cloak, she unfurls it like a matador brandishing his cape, and on her wonder horn she plays a frenzied jig. Just as the goblins had turned her sister into melting ice, so Ida in turn churns and dissolves them into a dancing stream—all except her baby sister, who, crooning and clapping her hands, now emerges reborn from an enormous broken eggshell, like the world from the cosmic egg. Outside the cave the clouds have parted, the seas are tranquil, the sun has risen through the mist, and Ida, in her Marian-blue dress, kneels in front of her sister and raises her hands in a gesture of benediction, and for the first time in the story, and in a moment of bliss, she and her sister look at each other face to face, soul to soul, I to Thou.

Hugging the baby tight, Ida begins her journey home, following a path beside a stream, on the other side of which she sees the seated, silhouetted figure of Mozart in his white powdered wig playing a pianoforte in his little summer cottage and assuming the role of Ida's guardian spirit. As she enters the dark woods, however, Ida must still pass by menacing trees with clutching skeletal branches, as well as five mauve-gray butterflies that ominously flutter around her. But when Ida and her sister finally arrive safely back home, they see their mama, now magically released from her imprisoning trance, rising from her bower and holding out a letter she has just received from Papa. She reads it aloud to Ida as she puts her arm around her: "I'll be home one day, / and my brave, bright little Ida / must watch the baby and her Mama / for her Papa, who loves her always." And we observe baby sister sitting on the grass and petting the dog, which has turned its head around to look at Mama. Ida's wonder horn lies on the ground just behind her, the world is disenthralled, the spell is broken, and there are no goblins in sight, having vanished like the tail end of a dream.

"I FEEL IT in me—like a woman having a baby," Maurice had confessed to me when he was describing the early birthing pains he was experiencing with regard to *Outside Over There*. At that time, in 1976, he hadn't gotten beyond the first seven lines. Maurice didn't search for words, he awaited them.

Outside Over There is made up of 359 words, and it took Maurice more than one hundred drafts to complete. "I have a hostility toward books that aren't well written," he once remarked, "and because a picture book is such a beautiful poetic form, I feel it should be treated with utmost respect. I know that I wouldn't be an illustrator without words. I've never done a book that was any good unless the text excited me, and my own texts have to be very good, as far as I'm concerned, before I illustrate them."

While he was awaiting the words for *Outside Over There,* he began to think about the pictures for the book. He knew that he needed to show a young girl lifting and holding an infant, so he got together with a professional photographer who knew a nine-year-old child named Esme. They dressed her in an old-fashioned nightgown, and they "rented," as Maurice put it, a fourteen-month-old baby and placed a lampshade-like bonnet on her head. "It was really the only way I could ever get the proper feel for the bulk of a baby as picked up by a nine-year-old," he recalled. "There are realistic touches that just can't be fudged, and I wanted to get them absolutely right." However, the baby kept slipping out of the older child's arms, so the photographer covered the studio floor with large pillows and shot about seventy photographs.

About a month later, Maurice began work on pencil drawings based on the children's poses, but he didn't try to reproduce the children's faces. "I can draw a baby's face," he said, "but to get the eyes you can't make up that questing, vulnerable, sober, funny, judgmental expression. The eyes have to come purely from your imagination, but I also studied all kinds of baby books—feeding books, teething books, pictures showing baby reactions to what's going on."

He completed the drawings several months later and decided to show them to some of his friends. But as the Jungian analyst Marie-Louise von Franz once warned, "A writer should not show or discuss what he is writing with too many people. He usually knows when the work is in the delicate state of growth. Someone may say, 'Yes . . . very good,' but just that little hesitation after the 'yes' can rob you of your courage to go on. A hesitation in the response or a silly question may lame you. One may even criticize it one-self once the child has been born and there is a certain distance; but when it is half formed, you cannot talk about it." Maurice had in fact warned himself not to share the drawings, but as he later said regretfully, "You do it because you're human. And my friends' verdict was, 'Publish these: they're beautiful, you're never going to top them. Forget the paintings.' You're never prepared for that kind of reaction, and I always knew this was going to be a full-color book, but I couldn't go on. So I dumped out. And there was a six-month hiatus between the last drawing and start of the first color paintings."

It was during that six-month period that Maurice suffered his first major depression. As he revealed to *The Horn Book*'s Roger Sutton in 2003, "*Outside Over There* was the most painful experience of my creative life. I think I went over my head. I went into a subject I thought I had some knowledge of or some control over, as I did with *Where the Wild Things Are* and *In the Night Kitchen*. *Wild Things* was excavation work, but I got up and out in time, like a miner getting out just before the blast occurs. *Night Kitchen* was a deeper run, and that was troublesome. But I didn't anticipate the horror of *Outside Over There,* and so I fell down . . . I fell off the ladder that goes down deep into the unconscious. Herman Melville called it *diving.* You dive deep and God help you. You could hit your head on something and never come up and nobody would even know you were missing. Or you will find some nugget that was worth the pain in your chest and you'll come up with it and that will be what you went down for. In other words, you either risk it or you sell out. And I didn't think I could finish the book, I lost my belief in it, I didn't know what I was doing, and so I quit, I stopped the book right in the middle."

It was during those painful days that Maurice received a phone call out of the blue from the opera and theater director Frank Corsaro, a longtime Sendak admirer, who later recounted some of their conversation:

Corsaro: I'm calling to pose a question. Have you ever given any thought to designing an opera?

Maurice: I think you've got the wrong number, Mr. Corsaro. Opera? Me?

Corsaro: I'm perfectly serious!

Maurice: But why me? I write and illustrate children's books, I'm mired in kiddie-book land.

Corsaro: Mired or not, you've got to face the fact that opera is the biggest kiddie book in the world. Besides there's a debut for everything in the arts, Mr. Sendak.

Maurice: So—nu? Which one do you have in mind?

Corsaro: The Magic Flute. I'm going to be directing it for the Houston Grand Opera in 1980.

Maurice: Die Zauberflöte?

Corsaro: Why? Do you know another opera with the same title?

Maurice: Mozart's?

Corsaro: Who else's?

Maurice: Oy gevalt!

Corsaro: So—nu?

Maurice: Are you Jewish?

Corsaro: I will be by the end of this conversation!

Maurice couldn't believe it. "I was nearly having my second coronary on the phone while he was talking to me," Maurice recalled to Steven Heller, "and I agreed to do it. So right in the middle of *Outside Over There* everything turned Mozart." He added, "If anybody could prove to me that Mozart was God, I would believe in God forever, and I do believe in Mozart as though he were God."

The Magic Flute was Maurice's favorite opera, a work that combines a panoply of radically different elements: opera buffa, opera seria, singspiel, popular song, bravura aria, ritual chorus, and chorale. And the way Mozart synthesizes and reconciles the sacred and the profane, the serious and the comic, and the elevated and the popular suggests Sendak's own all-embracing powers to use and transform the most disparate kind of materials, from creators as diverse as Randolph Caldecott and Walt Disney, Albrecht Dürer and Winsor McCay, Mozart and Carole King. Mozart himself would, in fact, turn out to be Ida's guardian spirit in *Outside Over There*.

"I am stirred to life by my labor," Maurice once remarked, and while working on *The Magic Flute* his depression lifted and he was able to return to his book. He remembered that he had left Ida on page twelve in her mama's yellow rain cloak, and he completed the color illustrations at the end of May 1979. But he then started having a recurrent dream, one that certainly required no interpretation, in which he saw himself giving birth to a child that was immediately taken away from him, so he delayed turning in the artwork to his publisher. But shortly after his fifty-first birthday on June 10, he hired a limousine and accompanied his "baby" to Harper & Row, which published the book in May 1981.

Maurice had sent me an advance copy of *Outside Over There* two months earlier, and when I asked him if he would be willing to talk to me about it for a book about children's literature I was then working on, he said he would be happy to do so. "You saw me when the baby was first gestating five years ago," he reminded me, "and now it's finally about to be born." So in early April, he and I met up at my New York apartment to discuss the "new arrival" over a dinner of deli sandwiches. (Some things never change.)

"You once said, Maurice, that your stories come to you in bits and pieces of memories that don't seem related, but that something in you determines they *will* be related. So I was curious to know what were some of the elements that influenced you for *Outside Over There*."

"First," he replied, "was a children's book that I looked at when I was very young with a friend, a girl named Selma, who lived next door. It was a book, which I haven't seen since, about a little girl in a rainstorm. Selma read better than I did, and as we went through the book together, I was riveted by the pictures, which were thirties-type illustrations. And I remember a very wet street and a little girl in a yellow slicker that was way too big for her, and her reflection was upside down in the rain. I recall that vividly—you could see two of her. And she was very big and the wind blew up and it billowed her out and her umbrella went inside out and the sky was gray. It either frightened me or excited me, but I've never lost the image of that child, and that was the original Ida, whoever she is and whatever book that was. So it was almost an obsession, really, to recover that original child in that original book and do my own book about her. I didn't know why I had to do that, I just knew I had to."

"Recently," I mentioned to Maurice, "I was rereading *The Juniper Tree* [a two-volume collection of the Grimms' tales, translated by Lore Segal and Randall Jarrell and illustrated by Sendak], and in it there's a very brief tale called 'The Goblins,' in which a bunch of goblins steal a child out of a cradle and leave a changeling with a thick head and staring eyes in its place. And a friend of the grieving mother tells her to take the changeling into the kitchen, set him on the hearth, light a fire, and boil water in two eggshells, which will make the changeling laugh, and when a changeling laughs, the story tells us, 'that's the end of him.'"

"That *is* the seed for my book," Maurice said, "and the effect the story had on me was enormous, but I don't know why. And my illustration I did for that story—the giant baby being *heaved* by those little goblins surrounding that great mound of flesh, and that baby staring out . . . Somebody once remarked to me that he loved the picture, but he asked, 'Which baby is this? The normal baby or the changeling?' And that was funny, because you couldn't really tell—all babies are slightly idiotic and drooly-looking at the corner of the mouth—so it might have been the changeling baby. And the reason the eggshells appear in *Outside Over There* is mostly in homage to the original source. You know that you have a changeling after boiling water in an eggshell.

Illustration for the Grimms' "The Goblins" from *The Juniper Tree*

"And the other thing is music," he continued. "If you play an instrument and the baby begins to dance to it, you know it can't be your baby. And that's why Ida plays a wonder horn. The two ingredients that you check a changeling out with, eggshells and music, are both incorporated in my story. But what we're missing here—and I can't give it to you because that's where Freud drew the curtain—is *why*. What were these things, what did they mean, that they had to be so obsessively pursued and riveted into a book?"

"What about Wilhelm Busch's picture story *Ice Peter*," I asked him, "in which the boy Peter falls into a frozen lake and turns to ice? And when he's thawing out, instead of becoming himself again he dissolves into water— somewhat like the changeling and goblins in your book."

"You know, Busch's *Max and Moritz* was a big thing in my life," Maurice told me. "Max is the name of the boy in *Wild Things,* my name is Moritz in German, and Max and Moritz get stuffed in the oven just as Mickey does in *Night Kitchen.* But I wasn't conscious of *Ice Peter,* although I *was* conscious of the influence of one of my favorite childhood books, *Little Black Sambo,* in which the tigers, by running around the tree, melt into butter. I *loved* that. And here in *Outside Over There* the children dissolve into the ether by dancing frantically. That's the only possible association. Well, maybe there's one with the witch in the movie version of *The Wizard of Oz* who, when they pour water on her, just melts and dissolves. I went bananas over that scene when I was a child—her shrinking and shrieking and going 'Ahhhhhahhh!' And I also decided to give Ida a blue dress in homage to Judy Garland, because I was so moved by her the first time I saw the movie, when I was about ten years old. And Ida's yellow rain cloak was in part my homage to the Yellow Brick Road."

"You also once pointed out that the fact that there are five baby goblins in your book might have had something to do with your recollection of the

Dionne quintuplets," five identical Canadian sisters, born in 1934, who were the first quints known to survive infancy.

"Yes," Maurice replied, "but that was an unconscious thing. It was my sister, Natalie, who pointed out to me, when she looked at the page in *Outside Over There* showing all five baby goblins, that it was just like the old newspaper photographs of all the quintuplets lolling around—you would see them in sort of unwittingly sexy poses with their little bonnets, and whenever I heard on the radio that they had a cold, I remember getting very upset. And after all these years, I still can't forget their names—Yvonne, Marie, Cécile, Annette, Émilie. So I guess that did influence the composition of the five babies . . . but then again, there are five wild things and there are five Sendaks—two parents and three children. I think that if there are five members in your family, then the number becomes important. Five has always been a magic number for me."

"There are certain paintings and drawings that also seem to have influenced *Outside Over There,*" I mentioned, "in particular *The Hülsenbeck Children,* by Philipp Otto Runge, in which we see two older children looming surrealistically above a picket fence and holding on to the handle of a wheelbarrow in which an intensely staring baby is clutching a gigantic sunflower plant."

"Yes, my book jacket is a conscious homage to that painting," Maurice confirmed. "Look at the fence, look at the baby staring out and clutching part of the flower just the way Runge's baby does. There's no question about that."

"And with regard to this painting," I said, "the art scholar Robert Rosenblum once commented on 'the red-cheeked faces of children looked at neither as little adults nor as adorable pets, but as containers of natural mysteries.'"

"And that too I read after *Outside Over There* was started, so it was a great

LEFT: Philipp Otto Runge:
The Hülsenbeck Children (1805–06)

BELOW: Book jacket for *Outside Over There*

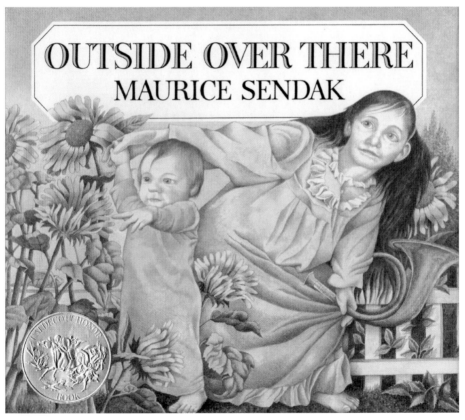

impetus—I felt I really had homed into Runge, and it was being confirmed by what Rosenblum was saying."

"I sense that William Blake was also an important model for you."

"Before I started working on the paintings for my book," Maurice told me, "I'd done pencil drawings that were so finished and powerful that I wasn't sure how to reconceive them in terms of color. And I really wasn't involved so much with Runge at that point. So I needed a clue—a color clue. I found the first in the film version of Eric Rohmer's *The Marquise of O.,* which was perfect in terms of time and setting . . . all the greens and mauves excited me. And the second was a visit to the Morgan Library, where I sat and looked through a magnifying glass at Blake's illustrations for Milton's *L'Allegro* and *Il Penseroso,* a suite of illustrations that I've always loved. At that period in Blake's life he was using an extremely controlled amount of colored stippling, like Seurat, though it only seems that way under magnification. And I simply grabbed hold of what Blake was doing technically and decided that I'd take a brush and, with a very fine infinitude of points of color, I'd stipple faces, clothing, everything. And that was a way of getting myself going.

"So the first illustrations I did are very stippled, and only after I'd gotten two or three pictures done did I start to relax, and I began to look at Runge, among others. The style of *Outside Over There* changes almost from page to page—it becomes much more secure by the midsection of the book, and much more purely mine. But the early illustrations are very strongly influenced by the stylistic effects of those particular William Blake pictures."

"The drawing of Ida playing her magic horn," I said, "reminded me immediately of Mahler's song cycle *The Youth's Magic Horn.*"

"Absolutely. That piece is based on songs collected during the same period in which the Grimms were collecting their tales, and for a similar reason: to get them all down before they disappeared. And it's my favorite period—the time of the Grimms, Clemens Brentano, a little bit of Novalis, and Kleist . . . although Kleist is slightly later. And I love the title *Des Knaben Wunderhorn,* and I love the songs—they're my favorite works by Mahler—so uninflated and unpretentious . . . And, of course, in that list I forgot to mention Mozart!"

"Mozart," I said, "really seems to be the overriding influence on your book, and he even makes an appearance in it as a kind of tutelary deity."

"Yes, *Outside Over There* is my attempt to make concrete my love of Mozart, and to do it as authentically and honestly in regard to his time as I could, so that every color, every shape is like part of his portrait. And whenever you do something for Mozart it automatically means you have to be scrupulously careful and honest. So this book is a concretizing of maybe the most passionately wonderful thing in my life. It's my *imagining* of Mozart's life, and it had to take this particular form. I sometimes think of it as an opera in pictures, and that's why after I'd designed the sets and costumes for *The Magic Flute* I cried during the performance, because I couldn't believe that I had been in the position of doing this thing with *him,* it was almost too much. But everything concerning Mozart is too much."

"In an uncanny way," I suggested, "both *The Magic Flute* and *Outside Over There* seem to resemble mystery rites."

"Yes," Maurice agreed. "I've taken many things from the opera for my book: the test of air—Ida floats; the test of fire—Ida underground; the test of water—when the goblins dissolve. These are all my variants on the opera. *Outside Over There,* of course, goes back to the 1930s, when I was sitting on a stoop with a little girl named Selma, so that everything else that has grown like Topsy over the years has been added to the project. But that I started to conceive of the book and that I would associate it with my favorite

Maurice Sendak's poster for the Houston Grand Opera's
1980 production of Mozart's *The Magic Flute*

work of art, and then that it should be so full of *The Magic Flute* before I, by luck, became a designer for a production of that particular work of art—it is incredible that it's all just a coincidence. Also, the fact that I did the opera right after *Outside Over There* is a miracle. It's like some kind of present to me for my having been brave, it's my medal of honor. Because the two go together. It sounds so vainglorious to suggest that this book is even anything like *The Magic Flute* . . . God knows, that's not what I'm saying. But thematically and in terms of what the opera means to me—just to me—is what *Outside Over There* is."

"Your set for *The Magic Flute* featured a cave," I pointed out, "and in *Outside Over There* a cave is the home of the goblins."

"The whole production of the opera begins in the Queen of the Night's cave," Maurice told me. "It's like the bowels of the earth, and Tamino is lying down and looking up at the sky. My view of *The Magic Flute* is that when Tamino and Papageno depart on their journey, they may leave in a balloon, but it's not because they're traveling a great distance; they're just two seconds away, as in a dream. In fact, everything happens just where they are, in that cave, but it's just that the scene changes. Things keep on unfolding, and it seems as if you've gone somewhere, but actually you've gone nowhere because you're always in the same place, you're in your head."

"So what you're saying about *The Magic Flute*," I remarked, "could in a way also be said about *Outside Over There*."

"That's absolutely true."

"Hearing you talk about *The Magic Flute* and *Outside Over There* in this way reminds me of the Greek philosopher Heraclitus's statement that 'the way up and the way down are one and the same,' and I imagine he might also have been referring to psychic space. And to me, this seems to be the space of both *The Magic Flute* as you conceive of it and of *Outside Over There*, where up and down, high and low, and inside and outside appear to exchange identities."

"I may be pushing it too far," Maurice responded, "but in a way my book is like a mirror reflection: it's called *Outside Over There,* but if you hold the title up to the mirror, so to speak, it says *Inside In Here.* You're right. And the whole construction of the writing, which is what I'm so proud of, gives the sense of being written backward. Some people may be disturbed by the construction of the sentences—they may be anxious to put commas in places like 'Ida mad' or 'Ida sly'—but the words are going their own strange route, and it's critical to the book."

"Unlike the texts for *Wild Things* and *Night Kitchen*," I said, "the text for *Outside Over There* sounds like a kind of incantation."

"The language in *Wild Things,*" Maurice pointed out, "is very erectile— ba-*room,* ba-*room*—it just pushes forward and then peters out, literally." He laughed. "But the language in *Outside Over There* is very perverse—as I said, it's going its own strange route. And *Night Kitchen* is exactly right in the middle between the other two books. And it's amazing that this triumvirate is perfectly formed."

"Some of the words in *Outside Over There,*" I observed, "can have one of several functions in a sentence, and sometimes one's not sure how they should be taken, like 'To rock the baby still.' It's as if the words aren't sure of their place."

"People," Maurice told me, "are desperate to place commas in places like 'Ida mad,' thinking that it should read 'Ida, mad' or 'Ida was mad,' but once you know the shape and geography of this book you'll know just where the punctuation has to go or doesn't go. There are odd constructions, but they're all intensely meant, because I wrote them nine million times. The language is compressed, but the pictures open them up. There's a counterpoint going on here like crazy. It's like a heartbeat—the words contract and the picture opens them up. And one of the clues to the book's meaning is to reverse everything that happens. I mean, Ida has to reverse things: only when her father tells her what to do in his song does she turn right side round and begin to solve the dilemma. Until then she's done everything wrong side round."

"You once mentioned how amazed you were when you discovered one day that the letters *ida,* when reversed, form the middle part of *Sadie,* the name of your mother."

"And that fact both chilled and delighted me, and verified forever the devious machinations of the unconscious."

"Halfway through the book, of course," I said, "Ida, instead of flying looking down and ahead, looks up and goes in the opposite direction."

"Yes, by going backward she made a serious mistake. She went backward out the window into outside over there."

"But how else, if you want to go back in time, can you go unless you go backward?"

"Well, you've got to puzzle that one out. Nothing is as easy as it looks. Backward has its price, even though that seems to be the right direction."

"I suppose I felt Ida was trying to get back in time as well as trying to get to some place."

"That could be," Maurice said, "but my point in this book is that nothing is as simple as it seems—what else have I learned from therapy and from all these difficult years? When you say that something is happening in the book, that may be true, but something else is occurring at that moment too. And the book is full of choices—is *that* why that happened? Or is *that* why that happened? Or, in fact, is it *all* of those reasons why that happened?"

"Several actions are occurring at the same time," I noted. "For instance, while Ida is doing something, the goblins are planning their kidnapping. Things happen, as you say, contrapuntally."

"Yes, there are two stories going on—Ida's story and the baby's story. Anyone who thinks the baby is a passive, inert creature doesn't appreciate or acknowledge what infants are capable of feeling. There are two separate books here. So when you know that, you know that anything that's happening is not happening just to one person but to two people, and it complicates things."

"Couldn't one perhaps imagine that Ida and the baby are two parts of the same person?" I asked.

"In this case I would say that there are two stories and two people and not simply the psyche of one person. There really are two distinct cases and two defined histories and experiences being explored here, and they conclude in different ways, even though the book concludes in a single way."

"At the end you do get a feeling of stability, of being back home."

"That's what was specifically intended," Maurice said. "However, there's another way of interpreting the end too. A friend of mine who read the book said, 'I can't stand it. I mean, are you trying to tell me that this is a happy ending when the father's away somewhere and he's writing this letter that just dumps everything on Ida? I mean, what kind of happy ending is that?' 'But who said it was a happy ending?' I replied. I'm not admitting anything, but in fact it's interesting that my friend was offended by the father's letter. There's a certain irony there. The father's really assuming that a nine-year-old can take care of the baby and Mama. Is he suggesting that Mama can't?"

"I felt that throughout the book the mother wasn't really there and that therefore Ida had to take on the mother's role."

"Because her husband has left," Maurice told me, "the mother is lost in thought—maybe a bit melancholic—so she's of no help to Ida. But appearances aside, we are really looking at only a minute's worth of life, and if the mother is distracted for that minute, can we draw the conclusion that she's distracted or comatose?"

"She certainly seems that way to me."

"But isn't it just that she's unwittingly distracted, like any normal mother who at any given moment of the day gets distracted, and during that moment something happens to the child—bad luck, bad timing? My intention was to leave room for a break to occur. In every child's life it happens that at a critical moment the mother—unbeknown to her that this *is* a critical moment—is inattentive to the child. And the child's then given his or her opportunity to make out for him- or herself, because there's no mama there . . . and there's also the impulse in the child to *be* the mama anyway, to use this opportunity to see if he or she can do without her. So, yes, at that moment Ida takes over for the mother, but that doesn't mean that that's a permanent state of being."

"It's also interesting that *Outside Over There* is your first picture book in which you have a little girl as a protagonist—actually *two* female protagonists."

"Everybody in the book is female," Maurice declared. "The father isn't there, and the mother, Ida, her sister, and all the goblins are girls. Look carefully: they're all female."

"But you're forgetting about Mozart and the two sailors and the shepherd," I pointed out.

"That's true, but it's a female world. And to tell you the truth, I don't know what that means or why that's so, but I just know that it's as right as rain."

"A friend of mine," I mentioned, "said the yellow rain cloak with all of its pleats and folds and puffs reminded her of the labial whorls that you see in Georgia O'Keeffe's flowers. And I also have to say that in the amazing double-page dreamscape in which Ida is floating backward on the clouds she actually looks a lot like Bernini's sculpture *Ecstasy of Saint Teresa*."

"I agree. In that picture just look at the orgasmic expression on Ida's face, her teeth are shining, her legs are parted—something is happening to her. She's a primal child, and just look at her name—I didn't realize until after I'd completed *Outside Over There* that the first two letters of her name spelled 'id,' and that tells you something about what is happening."

"And if you'll pardon my mentioning it," I added, "in that same picture you see a shepherd lying with his back toward us, either sleeping or doing who knows what with his sheep!"

"Well," said Maurice with a laugh, "I have to remind you of the drawing I did for Randall Jarrell's book *Fly by Night,* in which David is flying naked, and also with his back turned toward us, into the gigantic face of a mother owl. And here he is again as an older person, his ass still showing, although he's now clothed, but he's grown up to be a peasant taking care of the sheep. Quite consciously I brought him back to *Outside Over There,* but now it's Ida's turn to fly."

"You once wrote: '*In the Night Kitchen* comes from the direct middle of me, and it hurt like hell extracting it. Yes, indeed, very birth-delivery-type pains, and it's as regressed as I imagine I can go.' But in *Outside Over There* it seems to me that you've gone back even further."

"Absolutely. It reminds me of that awkward scene in *Altered States*—which could have been an interesting movie—where at the end the hero's determination is to go back and back and back to the very origins of man. And he does, he almost succeeds, he turns into . . . I don't know *what* that psychedelic imagery on the screen was supposed to be, but he looks as if he's a fetus, a cell, a sperm . . . he's going and going, and his girlfriend sees this happening and she puts her hand into the void and pulls him back. And then, in the end, he accepts the fact that you'd best not look, because if you look that far into it you can never come back. And that was like a cartoon version of what I think I went through in this book."

"It sounds as if you allowed Ida and the baby to go very far back."

"Yes. Meaning me too. And the way Pamina in *The Magic Flute* says to Tamino just before the trial scene—and remember, she's been such a frightened girl, not knowing whether she's going to die, not knowing why Tamino hasn't talked to her, not knowing whether or not he loves her anymore—and at that point she says, 'Put your hand on my shoulder, even roses have thorns, my love will guide us through.' And why am I bringing this up? Well, she's almost lost her life, I mean she's nearly committed suicide. And who brings her back from the edge of the grave? Three genies . . . three children, three infants."

"It's strange," I interjected, "but in *Outside Over There* the babies are the goblins."

"But more important to this discussion than the fact that they're like the goblins or that they have infant bodies is the fact that it's almost as if Pamina's infant self or some part of her had remembered something crucial to living. And when she comes back after having been near death—having been revivified by three genies, three child spirits—she's more poised than she has ever been before in the whole opera, and she says to Tamino, 'I will lead you through the thorny roses.' I mean, she has that absolute assurance. And why? Because she has been somewhere, somewhere that is appalling, like that silly man in *Altered States*. She's looked at something that's nearly cost her her life, and she's come back, barely. But from having looked and just come back she's turned into the great woman she is at the end of the opera. So you can come to a kind of reductive assumption that to be that kind of person you have to go back, you have to look, and you probably nearly have to die. You have to take the risk of dying."

"Speaking of dying," I said, "there's a famous letter that Mozart wrote to his father in 1787 in which he says something quite extraordinary. 'As Death, properly understood, is the true goal of our life,' Mozart confided, 'I have made myself so familiar these past years with this truest and best friend of mankind, that his face not only frightens me no more, but is of the greatest comfort and consolation to me! And I thank God for having bestowed on me the opportunity (you know what I mean) of learning to know it as the key to our happiness.' And it's been suggested that that parenthetical phrase 'you know what I mean' refers to a Freemasonic initiation—a mimed death and resurrection—that Mozart underwent. Do you know that letter?"

"Are you asking me that question *seriously*?" Maurice exclaimed.

"What do you mean?"

"Well, one, of course I know that letter. And two, I *own* that letter! Didn't you know that?"

I was dumbfounded. "You must be kidding! How did you obtain it?"

"I sold my old age to get it. It's just a piece of paper that I keep in a special folder covered with plastic, and it's such a totally in-contempt-of-money thing to have because of the ephemera of it, but what else is money worth? To me, it's like having the Turin Shroud. That letter was the last one that Mozart wrote to his father, and every time I look at it and see the salutation—*Mon Cher Papa*—I can't stand it."

"What do you think Mozart was referring to when he wrote 'you know what I mean'?" I asked him.

"Because if he said what he meant," Maurice explained, "Maria Theresa [the Habsburg empress, who abhorred Masonic ideas] would have come and torn it out of the letter. He couldn't have put it into words. And in that letter to his father Mozart goes on to say, and I'm paraphrasing, If you think I'm fearful of knowing about your illness and your possible death—his father had been ill, hadn't written to him recently, and did in fact die a month later—don't spare me, because I understand these things. And Mozart continues: There is not a night that I do not go to sleep and think that I might not wake in the morning. And yet there is no one who will say that your son is a morbid person—I'm the most cheerful person in the world—but knowing this makes me cheerful."

"I know that you understand what he's saying very well."

"Of course. If I had died of a heart attack, which I almost did in 1967, there would have been no *Night Kitchen,* and my career would have ended with *Higglety Pigglety Pop!*—a book that's all about death. And even in a comic work like my musical *Really Rosie,* all that the characters talk about is death—the whole thing is a theme and variations on how many ways you can die."

"And Mozart died so young," I mentioned.

"Yes, when he was writing that letter he must have known that he was dying."

"For some reason," I said, "I've always felt that even when Mozart was young his body must have told him that he wasn't going to have that many years."

"Mozart was a very sickly child," Maurice explained, "and with the terrible diseases children contracted at that time, it's amazing he lived until he was thirty-five. Don't forget that the Mozart family had eight or nine children, and only two of the siblings survived—Wolfgang and Nannerl. Imagine, there might have been even a *better* Mozart in the family. But isn't it amazing that he was one of the two? It almost makes you believe in God . . . but not quite. Do you believe?"

"Not really," I replied, "but as Rabelais supposedly said on his deathbed, 'The farce is finished. I go to seek a vast perhaps.' "

"Well, one doesn't need to believe," Maurice reflected. "Or maybe I do believe and just call it all kinds of different things. I do have beliefs that are very firm and consoling, but maybe I'm fooling myself."

"In any case," I added, "it's like what you mentioned before about Pamina in *The Magic Flute*: 'You have to take the risk of dying.' As Jesus said, 'And whosoever will lose his life for my sake shall find it.' "

"That's basically it," said Maurice, "that's the beautiful point of it all. And in a sense, that's also the moral of *Outside Over There*."

"**THERE ARE TWO** stories going on in *Outside Over There*," Maurice informed me when I interviewed him in April 1981, "Ida's story and the baby's story." But when I asked him if he could tell me something about the latter's story, he declined to do so, saying, "I don't want to frustrate you, Jonathan, but I *can't*. If your tape machine weren't on right now, I would— but it will have to wait until we're walking on the street later on, after the interview is over."

So as I accompanied Maurice to his New York apartment on lower Fifth Avenue, he confided to me that *Outside Over There* was in fact based on the Lindbergh kidnapping case. In what became known as "the crime of the century," Charles Lindbergh, Jr., the twenty-month-old son of the aviator Charles Lindbergh and his aviator-writer wife, Anne Morrow Lindbergh, was abducted from the second floor of the family home in Hopewell, New Jersey, on the evening of March 1, 1932. Two months later the partly buried, badly decomposed body of the child, with its head crushed, was found alongside a highway four and a half miles away from the home, and two sections of the wooden ladder that had been used to enter the child's bedroom were discovered less than a hundred feet from the house. Bruno Richard Hauptmann, who would always proclaim his innocence, was arrested and charged with the crime, and after a two-year-long trial he was found guilty of murder in the first degree. He was executed by electric chair on April 3, 1936.

When I asked Maurice why he had decided to avoid mentioning this backstory when talking about his book, he responded, "To bring that case up in relation to *Outside Over There* would be dangerous, because if you start talking about the fact that it's based on a scandalous case of a dreadful nature, it's going to cause trouble for the book. I'm going to be very careful not to mention it for now, because I think it will adversely affect librarians and other people as well. I suffered through the controversies regarding *In the Night Kitchen,* and that took five years to overcome, so if I put a Lindbergh on this, it will cause problems because the book may be troublesome enough." And it was not until several years later that Maurice would begin to speak more openly about the Lindbergh connection and about why this case had obsessed him throughout his life.

"I was a very sickly child and wasn't meant to live long," he told Bill Moyers in 2004, "but when the Lindbergh baby was kidnapped I somehow knew that it couldn't die because it was a rich, gentile baby, it had blue eyes and blond hair, the father was Captain Marvel and the mother was the princess of the universe, and they lived in a house in a place called Hopewell, New Jersey, with their German shepherd watchdog and where there were nannies and police. Who could climb up into the room and take the baby out and nobody know? How defenseless could babies be even among the rich? My life hung on that baby being recovered, and if that baby died I had no chance, because I was just a poor Jewish kid. That's what I thought, and though this didn't make much sense, that was the equation."

Maurice was only three and a half years old at that time, but he recalled hearing Anne Morrow Lindbergh on the radio talking in a broken voice about how her baby had a cold and would the person or persons who took him please rub camphor on his chest and warm the milk for him. But the specific triggering event that ultimately traumatized Maurice for the rest of his life occurred two months after the kidnapping. As he would later recall it, he had gone shopping with his mother, who was holding his hand, and on their way home they passed by a newsstand, and Maurice vividly remembered looking up and seeing on the cover of the morning edition of the *Daily News* a blazing headline: **Lindbergh Baby Found Dead Near Home.** Although Maurice couldn't yet read the words, he beheld a hideous photograph of the decaying remains of the child amid a tangle of leaves, and the newspaper had printed an enormous arrow that pointed to the fractured skull. "I had the bad luck of seeing it," Maurice would later remark. "Children have Polaroid vision memory: I saw it, I took it in, and it stayed there forever," and he added, "That photograph only appeared in the first edition of the *Daily News,* because Colonel Lindbergh threatened to sue the paper if it wasn't removed from the afternoon edition. But I told everybody that I'd seen the picture, and finally it got to be the scandal of the family and they thought I'd gone nuts. They told me there was no such picture, stop talking about it, but it was always in my head, and now I would die—there was no question about it— because if the Lindbergh baby couldn't make it, how was I going to fare?"

Comparing himself to the Ancient Mariner, Maurice would throughout his adult life fix his glittering eye on all and sundry and speak endlessly about his obsession. At a party in New York he encountered Gabriel Heatter, the radio reporter and commentator. "He was the only celebrity I ever wanted to meet in my whole life," Maurice admitted, "and I rushed over to him—he must have thought I was totally out of my mind—and said, 'You're the guy who introduced Mrs. Lindbergh on the radio.' And he said, 'Yeah.' But he had obviously introduced millions of people, so he couldn't fathom why I was so excited." On another occasion, Maurice attended an event where he found himself seated next to Reeve Lindbergh, Charles Lindbergh's youngest daughter, who also happened to be a children's-book writer—her fascinating memoir, *Under a Wing,* was published in 1998—and he leaned over to her and said, "I did a book—" and before he could finish his sentence, she looked at him and replied, "And it's called *Outside Over There,* and it's about my brother, isn't it?" According to Maurice, Reeve confessed to him that her parents hadn't wanted her to know anything about the case, so out of loyalty to them she had avoided reading about it. And Maurice asked if she now wanted to know about it, and she said "Yes," so he then and there told her the story about her little brother.

Maurice even went so far as to convince a friend to drive with him one evening to Hopewell, New Jersey. When they arrived there, he said that he was going to walk to the house. "No, no, no," his friend exclaimed in alarm. But Maurice was determined, and as he later recounted the incident, "It was seven o'clock, and we parked, and as I walked to the house I could hear people talking inside and dogs barking. And I thought, This is how it must have been! People are talking in the house, like the colonel and his wife on the first floor. And I then walked around the corner and looked up at the nursery window and thought, I would have had all the time in the world to put a ladder against that window. I went through the whole madness."

Over the years Maurice read innumerable books and magazine articles devoted to the Lindbergh case, collected Lindbergh kidnapping memorabilia, and attended many lectures about it, but his obsession with it was hardly his alone. On the popular Lindbergh Kidnapping Hoax Forum and the Lindbergh Kidnapping Discussion Board websites, kidnapping skeptics and debunkers assert that the crime of the century was not a kidnap/murder but rather the execution of an innocent man, and some of them wonder whether Charles Lindbergh himself—a "sadistic prankster and eugenicist," as one person called him—didn't in fact stage a kidnap hoax in order to cover up his own sinister participation in his son's mysterious disappearance, disposing of him and then framing Hauptmann, thereby allowing an innocent man to die for a kidnapping that never happened. But others have claimed that there was indeed a kidnapping and that it involved the family butler, Oliver Whately, while another theory has it that Lindbergh's sister-in-law, Elisabeth Morrow, killed her nephew in a jealous rage over having been spurned by the aviator.

With *Outside Over There,* however, Maurice finally woke up from his own personal Lindbergh nightmare. In the process of working on the book, he experienced what he described as a "mental collapse," confessing that he had "fallen off the ladder that goes down deep into the unconscious," but by climbing back up and completing it he confronted and conquered the inner goblins that had kidnapped his childhood soul. As he described the process to me, "The dissolution of the goblins in *Outside Over There* is the eradication and conquest of fear and depression, of hallucination, of neurosis—breaking through and making them literally disappear by one's own act—and through one's own perseverance one destroys an obsession." If you look closely at the bottom of the double-page dreamscape in *Outside Over There* you will see Maurice's photographically accurate portrait of little Charlie Lindbergh sitting alone in his underworld cave, alive and well; and as he would later confess: "*Outside Over There* became my exorcism of the Lindbergh case. In it, I am the Lindbergh baby and my sister saves me."

In a sense, his book also saved Maurice himself, and upon its publication he told *Publishers Weekly,* "*Outside Over There* is a release of something that has long pressured my internal self. It sounds hyperbolic but it's true: it's

ABOVE: From *Outside Over There*

BELOW: Photo of Charles Lindbergh, Jr., at his first birthday party (1931)

like profound salvation. Only once in my life have I touched the place where I wanted to go, and no other work of art has given me this inner peace and happiness. I have caught the thing that has eluded me for so long, so critical for living, and knowing that means everything, regardless of what anyone else says about the book. I'm not a happy man, I'm notorious for that. *Outside Over There* made me happy."

Part Four

I'm not against psychology or analysis," Maurice once told me. "I'm sure that the things I draw—little boys flying and falling—reveal something. In one sense it seems very obviously Freudian, as if coming out of my own analysis. People fear that artists who are analyzed are going to be stone-cold dried up and that the whole thing that makes them artists is going to be 'fixed' or castrated, but it's just the contrary, in my opinion. Analysis in fact gives you wonderful clues and cues as to what you're doing, and surely the fact that a large part of my twenties was spent on an analyst's couch enriched and deepened me and gave me the confidence to express much that I perhaps might not have without it."

In the fall of 2013, I happened to come across an enlightening essay published in 2008 by the New York psychoanalyst Dr. Richard M. Gottlieb. It was entitled "Maurice Sendak's Trilogy: Disappointment, Fury, and Their Transformation Through Art," and in it Gottlieb wrote about Sendak's unusual ability to gain access to and represent in words and pictures such things as the childhood fantasy of treating loved persons as food; the rages children feel toward the very people whom they love and depend on; the transformation of these rage states through the exercise of a child's creative imagination; and children's extraordinary capacity for resilience, survival, and the overcoming of adversity.

In the fall of 2014 I contacted Dr. Gottlieb, who is a faculty member of the New York Psychoanalytic Institute, where he has long taught courses on Freud's case histories. He is also an associate editor of the *Journal of the American Psychoanalytic Association* and the founding president of the Berkshire Psychoanalytic Institute. I asked him if he might be willing to talk with me about *Where the Wild Things Are, In the Night Kitchen,* and *Outside Over There,* as well as about Sendak's work in general. He generously agreed to do so and invited me to come to his Upper West Side office in Manhattan, where I sat on his analyst's couch and conversed with him over the course of several hours.

I first asked him how he had become interested in Sendak's work.

"A friend of mine in medical school gave me a copy of *Higglety Pigglety Pop!* as a present," he told me, "and it immediately became one of my favorite books."

"What was it that you liked about it?"

"What really hooked me initially was the whimsy and the magic and the mystery of it, as well as the drawings, which were so powerful and evocative of the Northern Romantic tradition and which evoked for me Ingmar Bergman's film *The Magician.* And I later found out that the model for the book's heroine, Jennie the dog, and Sendak's mother had died within a year of each other, and Sendak was broken up about it, and *Higglety Pigglety Pop!* was an expression of his grief about those losses. And I'll always remember that beautiful line that Jennie writes to her old master at the conclusion of the book: 'I can't tell you how to get to the Castle Yonder because I don't know where it is.'"

"And how did you happen to move on to the Sendak trilogy?"

"At that time I was reading and writing about cannibalistic fantasies common during childhood—the wish to eat and be eaten—and I moved on to *Wild Things* and then to *Night Kitchen,* which both had cannibalistic themes in them—Max's threatening to eat up his mother and then the wild things threatening to eat Max up as well, and then there was Mickey's close call with being cooked in the Mickey-Oven."

"In addition," I mentioned, "there's the fantasy sketch in which the child swallows his mother, and in the *Nutshell Library* there's the lion that eats Pierre."

"Yes," he said, "it's that fantasy of devouring and regurgitating. I think that Sendak was one of those people whose furies and maternal longings were both primarily configured as cannibalistic."

"How did you finally discover *Outside Over There?*"

"I had read an interview with Sendak in which he talked about his trilogy, and I have to admit that I didn't get *Outside Over There* right away. We all know that of the three books people tend to stay away from that one, and they say that it isn't popular because it's so dark. But I eventually came to think that in certain ways it's actually more subtle than *Wild Things* or *Night*

Kitchen. It's just that it's a little bit more difficult, like a difficult poem that you've got to work with before you can figure it out. Or like a complex new piece of music that you don't get the first time you hear it."

"Sendak," I noted, "once remarked that the three books of his trilogy were 'all about one minute's worth of distraction: one noise in the night kitchen had Mickey doing a weird thing; one temper tantrum, one wrong word, causes all the wild things to happen; and one minute's dreamy distraction allows the kidnapping in *Outside Over There* to occur.' But in your essay on the trilogy you suggest that what also binds these three works is a child in a rage."

"That's right," Gottlieb said. "Rage is absolutely central."

"The famous first line of Homer's *Iliad* reads: 'Rage—Goddess, sing the rage of Peleus's son Achilles,'" I said. "In a way, don't you think that one could also say, 'Rage—Sendak, sing the rage of Max, Mickey, and Ida'?"

"I do. Take Mickey: We first see him standing up on his bed and he's screaming 'QUIET DOWN THERE!' And there's a big speech bubble coming out of his mouth—if he's three feet tall, then the bubble looks as if it were six feet tall, so to speak. Mickey is unmistakably furious, but you don't know exactly what he's angry about. Maybe it's the Sunshine Bakers, who are making a racket downstairs. Sendak himself said that when he was a child he got angry because all he wanted to do was stay up and watch the bakers making their bread while he was forced to be in bed. And that's what Mickey's angry about too."

"It's always seemed to me," I suggested, "that Mickey may in fact be enraged by his parents making love in their bedroom next door. The primal scene."

"Yes, the first thing that might come to mind is the parental intercourse. I actually came across one of Sendak's preliminary drawings for this book in which you see Mickey floating by his mother and father, who are embracing in bed, and that certainly supports this idea. And you know, from a psychoanalytic point of view, Freud himself suggested that because the child doesn't understand sexual intercourse, he possibly views it as the father beating up the mother, a kind of sadistic act. But in a larger sense, the important point is that these kinds of displays of parental affection *exclude* the child, and this can be shattering to a child who believes or wishes to be the absolutely unparalleled and unrivaled apple of his mother's and father's eye. And suddenly there's a confrontation with the reality that he may be peripheral to the bond that goes on between the parents, so that he becomes just a third wheel. That can involve an enormous rage in the child, for some more than others."

"In this regard," I said, "the psychotherapist Adam Phillips observed that what we call rage might be 'the first stage of some process of enlightenment. The dispelling of a primal illusion. The simple and clearly unavoidable acknowledgment that there are other people in the world. Rage as our first tribute to otherness, both the otherness within and the otherness without.' And Phillips added, 'We may be childlike in our sexuality, but we are truly infantile in our rage.'"

"Sure, that's Mickey's rage," Gottlieb said. "Not only do I agree with Phillips, but he puts it very well. And I think that that's the idea that most informs *Night Kitchen*: 'I love my mother, I love my father, but what is she or he doing with him or her?'"

"Sendak," I reminded Gottlieb, "stated that his book *Kenny's Window* was all about, as he put it, 'the outrageous rage you inflict on inanimate objects'—in Kenny's case, on his teddy bear, Bucky—because 'you don't dare inflict them on your parents or your siblings.'"

"And this becomes a huge problem for a child," he said, "but also, of course, for certain adults. You get enraged at the very persons you love—

you'd like to kill them, but you love them, the people upon whom you are utterly dependent."

"Sendak also contended that Max's rage 'engorges' him," I added. "Rage and anger truly feed on themselves. As they say, 'The sticks are burning in the fire that they feed.' Rage can really destroy a person."

"Absolutely, and that's what Sendak means when he says that Max's rage engorges him. And that saying you quoted to me is a much neater way of expressing what I was trying to suggest before, which is that a child has a problem when he's enraged and furious at his mother, because among other things, he experiences this rage as dangerous, since it could burn the very sticks that keep the fire alive, it can consume and destroy the very person the relation depends on."

"But I think that rage can consume oneself as well."

"And the word I've often used to refer to this—and it's not quite as strong as 'consume'—is 'disorganized.' I mean, how clearly do you think when you're in a rage?"

"It's as if you *become* the rage itself," I observed.

"Yes, it's like the rage of Achilles that you spoke about before. When he goes berserk after Patroclus's death, he's consumed with rage—he goes on a killing spree, like the people we hear about all the time in the news. And when you think of Mickey in *Night Kitchen,* he is threatened by the possibility of being baked and consumed by fire."

"But Mickey," I argued, "does have a lot of fun wallowing in the bakers' dough."

"Well, he has a lot of fun when he *escapes* from the dough and the Mickey-Oven, but up to the point when he's about to be put into the oven, everything is pretty terrifying. It's done in a kind of 'ho-ho-ho, milk-in-the-batter' kind of way, but it's scary—he's going to be cooked and eaten or burned to death, and the jovial Oliver Hardy bakers are singing the whole time. But it's only after he escapes and jumps into the airplane and gets on top of the milk bottle and goes 'Cock-a-doodle-do!' that he has a lot of fun."

"But he's not having much fun when he's feeling enraged at his mother and father," I said. "*Odi et amo,* wrote the Roman poet Catullus: 'I hate and I love.' It's an old, old story."

"But it's a bigger deal for a child who hasn't yet learned how to manage his rage states," Gottlieb suggested. "All children have rages—and we adults also have rages—so it's great that Sendak can tell it like it is to children, and that's a reason why his books appeal to them, as well as to the adults who read the books to the kids. But his additional genius is built upon his uncanny ability not only to reexperience and convincingly depict a child's rage but also, on top of that, to build another layer, and that layer has to do with the *management* of the rage. And that requires somehow transforming that rage into art by means of dreaming, daydreaming, fantasy, reverie, storytelling, music-playing, or song-singing—'Milk in the batter! Milk in the batter!' or 'Higglety Pigglety Pop! / The dog has eaten the mop!' So what I'm talking about here is the transformative power of a child's poetic function."

"Sendak once remarked that he was obsessed with the question of how children were able to survive."

"And Sendak's answer," Gottlieb said, "was that children survive when they exercise their creative imagination."

"Mickey's dreaming himself into the Night Kitchen seems to exemplify this poetic function, don't you think?"

"Absolutely."

"And Max really seems to exercise his creative imagination big-time."

"Absolutely. The mother says to Max, 'You're a wild thing,' and Max replies, 'I'll eat you up!' So she sends him to his room without supper, and the room starts to change—the walls become transparent, the trees start grow-ing, and everything that happens from that moment on until he comes back home is transformative. There's this wonderful fictional narrative that Max makes up."

"Sendak believed that fantasy is the best means children have for taming wild things."

"That's right," said Gottlieb. "As Max might have stated it, 'I start in my room, it turns into the woods, I go on a journey on a boat, I meet monsters, I defeat them, I come back, and I'm fed and loved.' That's a great story, and that story is an example of the poetic function I was talking about before. Of course, that's also a trope—that story is everywhere in Western literature. Think of Odysseus—he goes off to war, and on his journey back home he meets all kinds of monsters, defeats them, and is reunited with his wife, son, and dog."

"And maybe," I added, "Penelope has prepared a warm meal for him."

"At the very least a warm meal!" he said, laughing.

"In what way do you think Ida manifests her poetic function in *Outside Over There*?"

"Well, Ida has her magic wonder horn, and she follows the advice of her father when she hears his voice telling her to 'catch those goblins with a tune.' And that's how she actually defeats those goblins: she gets them to dance faster and faster until they turn into bubbles and disappear into a stream of water. So for Ida it's music. And it's interesting to remember that in Mozart's *The Magic Flute* that's exactly what Papageno does to the bad guys, the min-ions of Monostatos, when he enchants them with his magic bells and makes them dance faster and faster until they lose their power, and that defeats them. It's just like what Ida does with her magic horn."

"And Ida," I said, "has her own rage as well, because she's angry that she has to take care of her baby sister, just as Sendak's sister, Natalie, was angry at him because she was forced to take care of him when he was a child."

"And she's of course also enraged by the goblins," Gottlieb added. "But in fact I don't think it's a very distant leap to equate Ida's goblins with Max's wild things."

"It's interesting that there are five goblins and five wild things," I pointed out, "and in *Wild Things* a rumpus takes place, and in *Outside Over There* there's a hubbub."

"Ida's goblins are the equivalents of Max's toothy wild things," Gottlieb suggested, "and perhaps we could also say that just as Max becomes king of all the wild things, so, similarly, Ida becomes the queen of all the wild goblins. The wild things and goblins are both personifications, and both represent similar things. In Max's case it's an orally tinged rage. The wild things have really nasty-looking teeth and really long claws and they can devour and tear apart just about anything, and they represent Max's rage at his mother. With regard to Ida, I think that the goblins represent her disowned fury."

"Sendak," I said, "thought that what was actually going through Ida's mind was, 'I wish I didn't have a sister, I wish she were dead.'"

"And the goblins," Gottlieb explained, "are unmistakably a representation of Ida's repudiated emotions toward the baby—'It's not me who's destructive, it's the goblins!' But it seems clear that the goblins are doing exactly what Ida wants to do to that baby, which is to toss it out that window, to get rid of it."

"Sendak once admitted that Ida was actually based on Natalie, and he stated, 'I remember my sister's demonic rages, and I remember her losing me at the 1939 World's Fair. But I also remember that she loved me very much, but my parents were both working very hard and didn't have enough time, so I was dumped on her. And that's the situation in *Outside Over There*: a baby is taken care of by an older child named Ida, who both loves and hates the newcomer.' Which is exactly what you said about Ida and her baby sister."

"Yes, he's saying that art imitates life, and that his life imitates his art. Ida has her rage, but she's also a good little girl, and like all older siblings she loves her little sister and wants to obey her mother and father and take care of her. And you can see the grief and fury come together when she realizes that the baby is a changeling. She's enraged by the goblins and feels terrible

and Mama in the arbor,

and wants to repair and undo this terrible damage. On the other hand, she'd like to be rid of the obligation to take care of her sister and rid herself of the competition, as well as to be rid of whatever it is that has made her mother so emotionally unavailable."

"When I first talked to Sendak about *Outside Over There,* he told me that he felt that Mama was 'a bit melancholic,' but he later—and I think more accurately—used the word 'gaga' to describe her."

Preliminary sketch of Ida's mother and her children for *Outside Over There*

"And Mama," said Gottlieb, "is gaga because where is Papa, and when, if ever, is he coming back? And it's not clear to me in *Outside Over There* that he *is* 'over there,' and it's not clear that he's ever coming back. So he has some responsibility for the mother being all gaga and being the way she is, because she has to take care of two children by herself. She's a sailor's wife, she's a single mom."

"To me," I said, "Sendak's depiction of the mother appears to be a classic example of dissociation, a withdrawing from what one can't bear. As the psychiatrist Mark Epstein described it, 'The shocked self is sacrificed, sent to its room for an endless timeout.'"

"That's a nice way of putting it," Gottlieb agreed. "The mother is clearly depressed. In fact, I came across a preliminary sketch that Sendak made in which the mother is in a state of despair—her head is buried in her hands, and the two children are desperately holding on to her. And in *Outside Over There,* the mother is clearly in an altered state."

"In your essay on the Sendak trilogy, you wrote about the emotionally unavailable mother who can't or will not recognize her child's concerns or state of mind, and you described this situation as 'a malignant state of affairs with far-reaching consequences for personality development' and used the term 'soul-blindness' with regard to this. What do you mean by soul-blindness?"

"That term was first used by the psychoanalyst Léon Wurmser to describe something that can be seen over time in certain mother-child relationships, and it has to do with the mother who, not necessarily out of motives of malice, just doesn't get or understand her child, who doesn't have a sense of empathy with regard to what the child's inner life is, and who is blind to his or her soul. And that's a terrible thing to grow up with, because even when the mother is trying to be nice and express affection, it's off the mark, it betrays a total misunderstanding of what the child is about, and it can leave a child very confused about all subsequent relationships."

"In this regard," I said, "there's an extraordinarily painful and revelatory statement that appears in one of Sendak's journal entries. He wrote: 'Charlie Lindbergh, the Mush baby. I was never born, I was dead in my mother's womb, I was the ice baby—and my mother didn't notice that I'd been replaced. She could have done the magic trick to get her real baby back, but she was too distracted and I stayed an ice baby.' Sendak explained that Mush refers to Moishe, which was his Jewish name, so he seems to have identified himself not only with the Lindbergh baby but also with the ice baby in *Outside Over There*. I found what he wrote very disturbing. What do you make of this?"

"One of the things that happens to children of disturbed parents, or even undisturbed parents who do disturbed things to their children—and we know about this from what we know about abused children—is that somehow the child feels that he or she is the one who's at fault, that there's something the matter with him or her. So by Sendak's saying he's the ice baby, he's also, I think, saying that his mother was the ice mother, and I think that that's more than implicit in the story of *Outside Over There*. So his viewing himself as an ice baby is a way for him, in his struggle, to deal with having an ice mother. This is a very good example of soul-blindness, and in the way that so many children do, he takes the blame onto himself, as if to say, 'I'm the ice baby and that's why my mother rejected me.'"

"So Sendak is both the ice baby *and* the Lindbergh baby."

"I think so," said Gottlieb, "but we have to remember that Sendak was not a simple man—his views of the important people in his life were not simple or unidimensional. His mother was not *only* an ice mother who was depriving and who left him with a chronic hunger for his entire life. She was also at times gratifying. And so here you have two mothers and two babies—an ice baby and a loved baby. But certainly the mother in *Outside Over There* is an ice mother."

"The child psychiatrist D. W. Winnicott famously talked about the idea of 'good-enough mothering.'"

"Right. And with regard to Ida's mother, you certainly have an example of at least a temporary *not* good-enough mothering. And I say temporarily because there's a rapprochement at the conclusion of the book, there's a happy ending, just as there is in *Wild Things* and *Night Kitchen*. Max, Mickey, and Ida take their journeys, have their adventures, and then return home. In Ida's case, the return home is a victory lap: she's done it, and the baby looks really happy."

"I once was lost, but now am found."

"Exactly."

"But on the other hand," I pointed out, "when Ida's walking on the path home, you see five mauve-gray butterflies—the same color as the goblins—

fluttering around her, as well as some tree branches with skeletal fingers that are trying to clutch her."

"In a way," Gottlieb observed, "it's like the end of the first *Star Wars* film. Luke is chasing and finally shoots down Darth Vader, and his spaceship goes flying off somewhere, but the door opens and you can see that there's an escape pod, and Darth Vader is obviously in it. So you know there's still evil on earth, and that these guys haven't been totally defeated. And in *Outside Over There,* the goblins have been banished, so, yes, there's a victory, but the enemy hasn't been completely vanquished. They'll be back, or their influence will still be felt."

"One of the most striking things about *Outside Over There,*" I mentioned, "is the way Sendak begins and concludes the book. When you open it, you're immediately confronted on the half-title page with an image of Ida coaching her baby sister to walk, but as she does so she lets go of the baby's right hand. And in the last image of the book Sendak shows us Ida now holding on to both of her sister's hands. If Ida's floating out the window backward was, as Sendak tells us, a serious mistake, then don't you think one could say that Ida's letting go of her sister's hand was her *first* serious mistake?"

"I do," Gottlieb agreed. "Winnicott also wrote about what he called the failure of secure holding, of not being held well. And Ida is not only letting go of the baby's hand, but she's letting her move toward the goblin who we see sitting beside the fence."

"Sendak told me that in *Outside Over There* we're really looking at only a minute's worth of life. And in a remarkable essay, the book publisher Stephen Roxburgh made the fascinating suggestion that in the moment between the baby's first step and her second step, the entire story of *Outside Over There* has been told."

"It *is* a fascinating suggestion," Gottlieb said, "and it reminds me of

the film *An Occurrence at Owl Creek Bridge,* in which a guy's being hanged, but you don't realize until the end that the entire narrative has taken place between when they let the platform go and when his neck snaps. But your observation about Ida's not holding her sister securely is consistent with the entire story of *Outside Over There,* because Ida's mother is totally incapable of holding *anyone.* Holding is a metaphor for all the things a mother does in the early days and months of a baby's life, reflecting all kinds of feelings and emotions as she tries to recognize and meet the baby's needs. And neither the mother nor Ida is providing a holding environment—it's not going very well, and the father is far away as well. And in some versions of what happens in child development, the role of the father is to offer the child help in separating him or her from the mother."

"How does he do that?"

"By being present, and by offering a way out of the perhaps overly intense enmeshment between mother and child. A child needs an exit, or a partial exit, and the father can help to accomplish that."

"But perhaps the father really isn't that far away," I dissented, "because I'd argue that he's actually very present in his absence. Sendak said that his book was a kind of mirror reflection, and explained that if you hold the title up to the mirror, so to speak, it says *Inside In Here*. And one day I realized that if you remove the final 'e' from the word 'here,' you get the word 'her,' so it seems to me that the father is in a sense *inside* Ida. To me he's like the omnipotent but invisible patriarchal Jewish God, who communicates to Ida just as God did to Adam, as when he tells her to turn herself around so that she'll be able to find and confront the goblins."

"But you don't want to be too literal about this," Gottlieb said. "What is happening here? Is the father speaking to Ida from his ship? No. But perhaps he *is* part of her dream, and in that sense, yes, he must be inside her."

"And it's often said that you can solve problems in dreams," I added.

"Freud thought the most important thing about dreams was that they represented the fulfillment of a childhood wish. But of course many dreams do solve problems."

"I don't know what you'll think of this idea," I said, "but I sometimes imagine that in *Outside Over There* it's the mother herself who is dreaming Ida's story. And in her dream, Ida takes on the mother's role, puts on her mother's rain cloak, overcomes the goblins, and rescues the baby. By doing that, she somehow enables the mother to confront and dissolve her own inner goblins, which are her feelings of anger toward her husband, and perhaps her envy of both her daughters. So it seems to me that through this reparative dream the mother liberates herself from the spell that's imprisoned her."

"You can indeed see it that way," Gottlieb responded. "Freud himself noted that all the characters in a dream represent aspects of the dreamer. And as I mentioned before, the dream is often a creative solution to a fury. We don't see the mother in an overt fury, but Sendak does in fact locate it in Ida."

"Speaking of dreams," I continued, "I recently gave a copy of *Outside Over There* to a friend of mine, and she told me that after reading it she had a series of nightmarish dreams and that she would be wary of letting her two kids look at the book because she didn't think it was 'kid-friendly.' So if you don't mind my asking, I'm curious to know if you yourself would give *Outside Over There* to your child."

"Yes, I would. But would I leave it around for a four-year-old to discover on his or her own? I don't think it would be a terrible thing to do, but it wouldn't be my first approach to the problem. I'd want to read it and be there in order to answer or anticipate questions that might come up. I think that there are three poles to the reading experience triangle: there's the book, the child, and the child sitting on the lap of the adult, because what's really helpful is the containing function played by the adult. Otherwise the child will think, 'Oh, these horrible things will happen to me!' So it's important that the adult is sitting and enveloping the child and calmly reading to him or her about the wicked witch or the goblins, like the ones in *Outside Over There*."

"What you just said reminds me of John Lennon's song 'Beautiful Boy,' in which he tells his son to close his eyes and have no fear because 'the monster's gone / he's on the run and your daddy's here.'"

"That's what I mean."

"But are you answering the question I asked you as a parent or as a psychoanalyst?"

"Same answer. But of course children are different one from the other. If someone gave me the book as a gift to read to a child who was already terribly anxious and having nightmares and waking up at night and running into my bedroom, then maybe I wouldn't do it, because I wouldn't want to add kerosene to the flames. But if I had a child who had a calmer disposition, I wouldn't hesitate to do so."

I then mentioned to Gottlieb that shortly after *Outside Over There* was published in 1981, Sendak bemusedly reported that a little Canadian girl had sent him a letter in which she declared, "I like all of your books, but why did you write this book, this is the first book I hate. I hate the babies in this book, why are they naked, I hope you die soon!" and the girl's mother added a note that said, "I wondered if I should even mail this to you—I didn't want to hurt your feelings." But on the other hand the writer and editor Amanda Katz, who in 1981 was an older sister to a one-year-old boy who she said looked a lot like Ida's baby sister, stated that rather than having found *Outside Over There* "creepy," she felt it actually made intuitive sense, because, as she explained, "it was a vision of the world that by the end of the book was not only comforting but also somehow illustrative of how to be responsible, of how to be brave, of how to live surrounded by the incomprehensible."

"And that's exactly what I was saying when I told you that kids are different from one another," Gottlieb responded. "Those are two very different kids."

"Sendak himself," I added, "once wrote: 'People say you mustn't frighten children, but you can't, because they're already frightened, they already know all these things. All you can do is console them.'"

"Yes, Sendak is trying to counter the argument that his books are toxic to children because they scare them about things that they didn't know about and that they're somehow planting these scary ideas in their minds. And his reply is absolutely true: It's already there and I'm doing them a favor by giving them a chance to process it, because otherwise it gets all the more camouflaged."

I then quoted to Gottlieb the educational psychologist Nicholas Tucker's statement that "children produce their own horrific fantasies and nightmares, which may be about anything from murder to mutilation to incest or cannibalism, whether they have read frightening books or not." And Tucker added, "Like Rumpelstiltskin, frightening things lose a lot of their power when they're brought out into the open and named. So books that don't ignore frightening topics but give them their place can help rather than corrupt children."

"That's really good," Gottlieb remarked, "and I should add to this that because Sendak was in touch with these things and was able to speak about them and render them visually, his books have an enormous appeal to children who resonate with this truth."

"Sendak," I noted, "once remarked that 'you must allow that children are small, courageous people who deal every day with a multitude of problems, and what they most yearn for is a bit of truth.'"

"But we should also remember that his books are at least first read to children by adults," Gottlieb pointed out. "And you can bet that adults do so because they too resonate with that truth. Sendak's books resonate with aspects of *us* as adults, and particularly when we're close to children when we read to them. Kids are sitting in our laps in a very intimate connection to us, and we're looking at pictures together, so it's a very powerful experience. And as I mentioned before, the situation is that of a mother or father with a young child on her or his lap, or, as I used to do with my kids, sitting on the bed with them, and we're looking at a book together that is often so powerfully evocative of every kind of pleasurable body experience, which many of us have to repudiate as adults because it's the cost of growing up."

"Adam Phillips wrote that some psychoanalysts today, as he put it, 'drift toward a disavowal of the sensuous pleasures of childhood, and in their commitment to the child's future they forget his bodily beginnings.'"

"But Sendak certainly didn't," Gottlieb said.

"So let's say you're reading *In the Night Kitchen* to your kids," I proposed. "How do you deal with the fact that Mickey is flying around naked?"

"I think that if you overemphasize the nakedness of the boy, you miss the importance of the flying aspect. Sendak said he believed that when you dream, you're naked in that dream."

"Do you think that's true?"

"I don't know if that's always true. But it's hardly deep psychological theory to relate images of flying to elation, which is the opposite of depression. Flying can have an erotic component, but I think that Sendak is mainly concerned with this wonderful feeling of bliss."

"Sendak once declared, 'I'm in recovery from my childhood.'"

"But how do you recover from your childhood?" Gottlieb asked me.

"I don't know. How do you?"

"Well, you don't need to recover from your childhood bliss, you just need to recover from your childhood rages."

"If you had to choose one aspect of Sendak's work that particularly resonates with you," I asked him, "what would that be?"

"Max staring into the wild things' yellow eyes without blinking, and Ida fearlessly confronting the goblins," Gottlieb answered. "And that's a lot of what I try to teach my patients to do—stare unflinchingly at the aspects of themselves that they've previously been unable to look at *without* flinching."

"Doesn't that require a lot of willpower?"

"Willpower and courage, and maybe for some people it requires a guide—and that's what a therapist sometimes is, someone who's accompanying you on a journey."

Part Five

The Swiss psychoanalyst Carl Jung suggested that "an artist's work takes on a life of its own, and it outgrows him, like a child its mother." So in the spring of 2015, in order to gain a Jungian perspective on *Outside Over There,* I went to see Margaret Klenck, who is a Jungian analyst in private practice in New York City and the past president of New York's Jungian Psychoanalytic Association, in order to have a discussion with her about Sendak's then thirty-four-year-old child.

When I arrived at her Upper West Side office, I mentioned that Sendak had spoken to me about having given birth to *Outside Over*

There but had also remarked, "When I was dreaming *Outside Over There,* what I was imagining was the most real thing I've ever felt. It seemed as if nothing that would occur after it would be as real or as intensely wonderful." Dream interpretation was one of Jung's most significant contributions to modern psychology, and I remarked to Klenck that *Outside Over There* really felt like a dream to me.

"It really does," she agreed, "and perhaps today we can walk through it, look at the images, and see what meanings emerge from them."

"The psychologist James Hillman," I said, "once asserted that for a dream image to work in life it must, like a mystery, be experienced as fully real."

"Well, all images are real," Klenck observed. "We're all made up of images—psyche is image—so maybe what Hillman is talking about has to do with whether or not those images can be useful for us. And dreams are real, they're really happening, but they're just happening on a different frequency from waking life."

"And Henry David Thoreau," I mentioned, "declared that 'our truest life is when we are in dreams awake.' I find that such a beautiful statement."

"It's beautiful," she responded, "because it *is* true. Jung said that dreams are working whether we're conscious of them or not. They're always sending what we're not conscious or aware of in order to rebalance things, and if we become conscious or aware of what that message is, then we can really use it and be transformed. And *Outside Over There* is so much about the pull to unconsciousness, the pull back into the Great Mother, the pull away from differentiation."

"In what sense?" I asked her.

"There's always a tension between that absolute ouroboros-like bliss, where there's no differentiation between you and the universe, and consciousness, where there's always differentiation. As soon as you have a thought, things start to divide into two: both/and, either/or—"

"Outside/inside."

"And we need that differentiation to be conscious," Klenck asserted. "In *Wild Things* and *Night Kitchen,* for example, Max and Mickey are on their own adventures, they're discovering their heroic qualities, they're individuating. But Ida's not—she's beginning to have a little bit of a personality, but as a dream figure she's *compelled* to save her sister, because her mother isn't going to do it."

"Because the mother's really unconscious."

"Yes," she said. "If *Outside Over There* were one of my patient's dreams, one of the things I'd work on with the patient is the feeling one gets at the end that there's still no father."

"In his letter to his wife and children," I noted, "the absent father writes: 'My brave, bright little Ida must watch the baby and her Mama for her Papa, who loves her always.'"

"But the father's still not and may never be there," Klenck remarked, "so in classic Jungian dream analysis we might say that right from the outset there's no sense of the *masculine*—the father's away at sea, he's off on the great unconscious, and you're hoping that at the end some sense of the masculine is going to appear in order to rebalance things. Of course the mother's not there either—she doesn't even have a face when we first see her. However, and I don't know about you, I find that the exquisite drawings are voluptuously feminine. The mother's yellow rain cloak is unbelievably vaginal . . ."

"And all of those labial whorls look like Georgia O'Keeffe's flowers," I added.

"I was also really struck," she said, "by what to me looked like the fallopian-tube shapes of Ida's wonder horn—it's not a trumpet or a flute.

So there's nothing at all masculine at the beginning of this dream, there's a mother and two daughters, and the fourth element is missing. And we wonder, how is this going to rebalance? Is it in fact going to rebalance? Will it come back around? Will there be a fourth? Jung used to talk about the fourfold structure of the psyche, but here it turns out that there's nil. So this is not a traditional story, it doesn't resolve in a classical way."

"Sendak," I mentioned, "asserted that *Outside Over There* was 'a female world,' and pointed out that the mother, Ida, her baby sister, and all of the goblins are female. He declared, 'I don't know what that means or why that's so, but I just know it's as right as rain.'"

"And you can really feel that," Klenck said. "I think of this issue of the feminine as the ground of everything: it's the realm of the primal mother, the Great Mother, and there's no room for the masculine. And part of what I hear in Sendak's saying that it's as right as rain is that this reflects a profoundly early world, when everyone was in the womb, as we all were at one time. There's no father; he's outside over there. The 'other' is very far away, and the feminine world is all there is. And on one level it's bliss, but on another level it doesn't allow you to become who you're going to become because you can't leave."

"Could you say something more about this?" I asked her.

"The Jungian take on development," she explained, "is that at some point the ego starts to differentiate. And Ida begins to do so, she gets her will together, she tricks the goblins, she turns them into a dancing stream. And we all have those moments when we're just coming into consciousness. But at the end of the book, when the mother's hand is for the first time touching Ida, she's at the same time keeping her daughter there. Ida's stuck in this primary place—primal, pre-Oedipal, almost preconscious. And what's extraordinary about *Outside Over There* is that although it's a book about the mother world, it's one with no love and no relatedness, which is so mind-bending, because mother *is* relatedness, that's its primary function, and in this book there's only a little gasp of that."

"On the other hand," I said, "I have the feeling that when Ida passes through the window, that window becomes a kind of passageway or gateway into her mind or psyche, and this allows her to undertake an interior journey on her own, just as Alice does when she goes down the rabbit hole."

"It *is* the beginning of a heroic journey," Klenck agreed. "Ida does go through this portal, but she does so pretty unconsciously—she's not looking forward, she's falling backward—but still you could say that it is like a little birth."

"And in a way it's like what happens to Mickey when he dreams himself into the Night Kitchen, don't you think?"

"Yes, and now she's on her journey and she has something to do, and she's doing it, and it's dangerous and confusing, but she does start to awaken in this dream."

"She's now in a dream awake," I said, "and she rises to the occasion."

"She does, and the potential for a true life begins when she passes through that window. Up till then she's been mired in this mother world. But Sendak says that she's made a mistake by flying out the window backward. From his point of view it's a mistake, but from a Jungian point of view whenever you make a serious mistake—like Prometheus stealing the fire or Eve eating the apple—you're actually going to get something new. Making a serious mistake in a dream always results in something new, and for Ida, going through that window is the beginning of an interior experience that's separate from everybody else's. For the first time she's alone, and when she wakes up she's an individual. And of course it is the father's voice that helps wake her up."

"Recently," I said, "I read a fascinating article about James Joyce's daughter, Lucia, who was diagnosed as schizophrenic. Carl Jung saw and treated her for a short time and remarked that Lucia and her father were like two people going to the bottom of the river, but that one of them was falling and the other was diving."

"That's exactly what we were just talking about," Klenck reminded me. "Ida is *falling* out the window; she's not ultimately in control of it. She's not climbing out the window—that would be diving. Diving is when you have intentionality, the *willingness* to do something, not just having the *will* to do it. In analysis, if somebody isn't willing to change and get better, it won't work, but if you're willing to be different, to be relieved, something can happen. And Ida's not there yet. She's not diving, she's falling until her father's voice tells her to turn around and put her head in the right direction, and only then can she go into the cave and do all that great work with those goblins and rescue her baby sister. It's at that point that she makes the move from falling to diving."

"I mistakenly thought you said 'dying' instead of 'diving.' It must have been a kind of Freudian mishearing!"

"Yes," she said, laughing, "but in any birth is the death of the old."

"It's interesting," I pointed out, "that when Sendak used to speak about the creation of his trilogy, he often used the metaphors of diving and plummeting. 'In *Wild Things,*' he once said, 'I went deeper into my childhood than anything I'd done before, and *Night Kitchen* was a deeper run.' But he confessed that while working on *Outside Over There,* which he called 'the excavation of my soul and the last Sendakian archeological dig,' he experienced an emotional breakdown."

"One could say that developmentally Sendak went all the way back into the womb," Klenck suggested, "and that's as far as you can go. I mean, Mickey's closer to doing that than Max because he's into the milk, but that's still at the breast, you're already born. But *Outside Over There* is really a return to the womb, so archeologically Sendak went back through his childhood down into his earliest and most innermost place, and he had to go that deep in order to save the inner feminine."

"How did he do that?"

"He used the nine-year-old, innocent, feminine part of his being in order to rescue Ida's sister from the absolute merger with the Great Mother. Ida saves the baby from that fate, and maybe because of that, the baby will be able to grow up and have an independent life. I think that somehow Sendak's primary relationship to his mother made him have to work this stuff out in a very deep, feminine way, and in doing so he experienced his own anima, which is as deep as you can get."

"I gather that when Jung talks about the anima he's referring to the unconscious feminine component of a man's personality, just as the term 'animus' refers to the unconscious masculine component of a woman's personality. Is that right?"

"With regard to anima, that sounds a bit too personal," she replied. "That's like saying 'I like pink, so that's my feminine side.' No, it's way deeper than that, it's really soul stuff, and if soul is feminine, it's a way of relating to the world with receptivity, possibility, and creativity. And anima holds that kind of energy."

"When Jungians use the words 'feminine' and 'masculine,' are they specifically referring to female and male?" I asked her.

"No, because everybody has both of those qualities, everybody has receptive and aggressive qualities. It's not true that men are more *thinking* types and women more *feeling* types. When we use those terms we're actually talking about psyche, about soul."

"But is a man's anima figure always a female, and a woman's animus figure always a male?"

"We're now understanding through gender studies that it doesn't necessarily have to be female/male but it does have to be 'other.' It's what my colleague Morgan Stebbins and I refer to as the 'heated other,' the thing that is 'hot' in some way—intellectually, emotionally, sexually—that you encounter in yourself. Now it may be confusing when somebody is sexually and emotionally attracted to someone of the same sex, because then that person isn't as 'other' in waking life—there's a similarity. So the Jungian world is having to look at this phenomenon. But even in the classical Jungian vision of the anima—the feminine soul-piece of a man—the important thing is the *otherness.* Everybody has to make sense of their own sexuality, they have to have their own narrative about it, and with regard to Sendak, it seems to me that in *Outside Over There* something about his soul is female—as exemplified by Ida's innocent, free, and hopeful baby sister—and that soul gets saved."

"Sendak himself declared, 'In *Outside Over There* I am the Lindbergh baby and my sister saves me.'"

"Yes, I think that there was something about that innocent baby that was profoundly significant to what in Jungian terms we would call Sendak's 'Self,' to his sense of wholeness."

"Sendak," I mentioned, "told me that he had dreamed *Outside Over There,* and I know that many Jungians and mythologists such as Joseph Campbell have suggested that there are two kinds of dreams—the personal dream, which draws on the events and problems of one's own life, and the archetypal dream, which carries a mythic theme."

"But I think that every dream has both aspects," Klenck said, "because there's always an objective and a subjective layer of the psyche that are conversing with each other. In *Outside Over There* we're definitely seeing Sendak's personal story—his personal fears and demons, his personal struggle with his personal mother, his personal sister, his struggle with his own feminine—where that's going to be inside of him and what that's going to mean to him. All of that. He stated that his mother didn't mother him very well—and remember that in *Outside Over There* Ida's not paying attention to her baby sister—so how he mothers himself is the important question, and how he does so would be one of the things that would reveal itself in this book."

"Someone once asserted that great works of art restore the lost mother. Do you agree with that?"

"I think that they actually restore the lost *inner* mother," she responded. "It's the archetypal mother who's going to care for him. His self-care is now going to be internal, he's not going to look for it externally. So he now has an inner mother who is brave, attentive, and relational."

"Of course another significant thing about Sendak's personal *Outside Over There* dream," I added, "is the way in which it reflects his obsession with the Lindbergh kidnapping case, but it also made me think of the Greek myth of the goddess Demeter and her daughter, Persephone. The story goes that while Persephone was out one day picking a narcissus flower in a meadow she was kidnapped by the god Hades on his golden chariot and 'raped into the underworld,' which is what also happens to Ida's baby sister."

"But the baby isn't and can't be raped by the goblins," Klenck disagreed, "because they're babies themselves, which is very interesting. In the Greek myth, Zeus, who's Persephone's father and the brother of Hades, sets it up for her to get taken, just as in *Outside Over There* we have a father who's ultimately responsible for the baby sister's kidnapping. But once again the point is that in both cases they had to break up the dominion of the mother, because otherwise the girl doesn't grow up, it's just one, big ouroboric mom."

"Nevertheless, it's a pretty brutal story," I insisted.

"There's no question about that. She gets dragged down, but Persephone is curious about that narcissus flower, and in a way I think that the flower is a little bit like Ida's window, and both of their journeys that take them into the underworld are initiations into life and death."

"What really intrigues me about the Demeter and Persephone myth," I confessed, "is the remarkable way that it resonates with the story of Ida and her sister, and particularly as it manifests itself in the famous ancient Greek ritual that took place at the Temple of Demeter at Eleusis, where the female initiates took on the role of Demeter and descended into an underground sanctuary of clefts and chasms in order to symbolically search for the lost daughter. And in doing so they experienced the emotions of loss and grief and finally the bliss of reunion. So don't you think that Ida could be seen as taking on the role of Demeter and her baby sister the role of Persephone?"

"It's the perfect connection," Klenck replied. "And it amplifies the fact that Ida is taking on the role of the mother because the actual mother has withdrawn into a melancholy stupor."

"To me," I said, "*Outside Over There* seems to be a kind of Eleusinian mystery dream."

"It is, and like that mystery it's also a ritual."

"It's interesting that you used the word 'ritual,' because Sendak was working on a production of Mozart's *The Magic Flute* at the same time that he was creating *Outside Over There,* and the poet and critic Kenneth Rexroth once suggested that this Mozart opera, as well as Shakespeare's *The Tempest,* were self-contained mystery religions. It seems to me that *Outside Over There* also seems to convey the substance and feeling of such a mystery religion."

"Absolutely. I think it's really in there. And that would lead me to wonder if part of Sendak's creative process wasn't really invoking this kind of drama as part of his own anima ritual that attempted to retrieve the innocent feminine away from the destructive mother, as we talked about before, and that maybe this was something he had to go through every time he created something, wrote something, or drew something, in order to get in touch with his own creativity and to restore right order between mothers and children."

"James Hillman declared that when one analyzes a dream one should always, as he put it, 'engage the image' and 'let the image speak.'"

"That's the Jungian way," Klenck affirmed, "and that's one of the big ways that Jung and Freud differed. We don't interpret so much, we're more interested in translating the image into psychological language, so, for example, a cave is a *cave.* When Jung and Hillman talk about sticking with an image such as that of a cave, they mean what's the archetype embedded in the image, what's the dominant of the image, what amplifies out of that image?

Or put it another way: What is essentially true about that image? What are the specific attributes of a cave, or a stream, or a dog, or a mother?"

"In *Outside Over There*," I noted, "a cave is the home of the goblins, and the cave has often been thought of as the womb of Mother Earth, a place of burial and rebirth and of mystery and renewal. And in *Outside Over There* it's the place where Ida finally discovers her lost sister."

"Yes, that's all in there. And I don't remember, but does the moon appear in that recognition scene?"

"No, you just see the sun rising through the mist."

"Ah! And that's because there's consciousness; the little oil lamp that we've previously seen in the book has now become the sun. It's as if Ida were saying to her sister, 'Oh, that's you! Oh, that's you! Oh, we're separate! We're still in the womb, we're still in the egg, but it's open now.' And that's consciousness. Recognition is differentiation."

"In this recognition scene," I said, "we see the baby emerging from an egg. So could we say that this signifies death to the old life and rebirth to the new?"

"There's a potential for it. With regard to the baby there is, and perhaps also for Ida, although as I mentioned before, at the end of the book her father is telling her that she still has to take care of her mother and sister. But at least for now, her agency and her saving the baby bring all kinds of new energies into their lives, and that is definitely transformative."

"The writer Harold Goddard," I said, "wrote a beautiful essay about the poet William Blake in which he stated, 'The moment when a chick pecks its way out to the light is the moment when the water-lily opens to the sun, and both correspond to the birth of the Imagination.' And I felt that this could also apply to that recognition scene."

"Well, image and imagination are the same thing," Klenck told me, "and in fact the psyche is made up of images. Everything is an image: language, pictures, sounds. The minute we have consciousness of any of these things, we can create—we can discover patterns and make something of them. So that's why the recognition scene between Ida and her sister is so hopeful: this is the blessing, this is image and imagination. Imagination is our *materia*: I can imagine with you, we can do something, we can create together. And for Ida and her sister there's the beginning of an imaginal relationship—they can finally play together because there are two of them now. And I imagine that for Sendak this was an extraordinarily healing image."

"And in *Outside Over There,*" I reminded her, "Sendak has symbolically rescued the Lindbergh baby."

"Yes, he's been saved. And we could say that the baby is Sendak's Self-image. He's in the depth of his imaginal world, and his anima has led him to this image and saved it. For Ida, she actually begins to love her sister, the sister finally gets seen. And for the reader . . . I don't know how you feel, but I feel, Hurrah! Because Ida and her sister can both come out of this birth canal now, they're born. And the reader is also going through this journey and is using his or her imagination to *feel* it. This image is so flooded with feeling."

"Speaking of flooded," I said, "water with all its purifying and regenerating powers is also a significant image in *Outside Over There*. And there are two powerful water images here. The ice baby melts and turns into water, and all that is left of it is a little yellow cap and two hands. And then Ida liquefies and dissolves the goblins. So the goblins dissolve the baby and then Ida in turn dissolves the goblins."

"They return to their natural, elemental state," Klenck agreed, "and they don't have to be goblins anymore. Goblins are traditionally trickster messengers of the Great Mother—they come out of the earth, they live in caves, and now they've gone back to a less differentiated aspect of nature, or the Great Mother."

"Sendak confided to me that in *Outside Over There* he was able to dissolve his own inner goblins, and by doing so he declared that he had eradicated and conquered his fears, neurosis, depression, and obsession."

"This really resonates with me," she said, "because when I first read *Outside Over There,* I immediately felt that the goblins were the agents of the mother's depression, and this depression was destroying any possibility of relatedness, new life, and imagination. And Sendak overcame his own depression in this book, just as he overcame the anger he felt toward his mother in *Where the Wild Things Are.*"

I remarked to Klenck that the moon was one of Sendak's most abiding obsessions, and that it accompanies and guides Max, Mickey, and Ida on their journeys and is a protective, maternal presence in almost all his books. In *Higglety Pigglety Pop!* the moon turns into Mother Goose, and Sendak provides her with the face of his mother, Sadie; and in *We Are All in the Dumps with Jack and Guy,* which tells the story of a group of homeless boys, the moon actually appears three times in one of the illustrations. After reading that book, a young girl sent Sendak a letter in which she told him that to her the book meant that "the moon is everybody's mother," and Sendak avowed that "it was the best review I ever had—it was as if that girl dropped her plumb line right into the heart of the book."

"The moon is the nighttime," Klenck responded, "it's the darkness, it's the unknown. And the mothers are so unknown. They're *unknowable,* because we encounter them before we have the capacity to know anything. They're in charge of us before we even know that there's an us. Fathers, no matter who they are, are never as mysterious as mothers, because we only meet them when we're born. But we've already had nine months of being completely engulfed in and enveloped by the mother, breathing the same air, hearing the same heartbeat. Mothers are an absolute mystery, and everyone's journey is out of the mother to become their own being and then being able to relate to other persons."

"So maybe that's why there's the sun god and the moon goddess."

"Yes, because the moon is reflective, it doesn't have its own source of energy. If you've ever been out in the wilderness, the only way you can see in the dark is when there's a moon. The only way you can see anything when you're in deep unconsciousness and darkness is with the reflected light from the sun. At night you need the moon."

"In her book *Woman's Mysteries,*" I mentioned, "M. Esther Harding noted that while the sun is a constant and reliable source of light and heat, the moon is changeable, and she observed that the moon goddess was dual in her very nature and lived her lives in phases. In the upper-world phase, corresponding to the bright moon, she was good, kind, and beneficent, but in the dark phase she was cruel and destructive consciousness."

"And that could in a way be describing Sendak's mother," she agreed. "You can rely on the moon only by acknowledging that it's going to keep changing."

"Speaking of the cruel and destructive," I said, "the most potent image in *Outside Over There* is certainly that of the faceless, hooded goblins, and to me they represent what Jung referred to as the 'shadow.' How would you describe the shadow?"

"The shadow is what you've cast out and disowned," Klenck explained. "Shadow is all the stuff that consciousness has rejected so that you can stay adapted to your environment. Anything that you, your family, your culture, or your religion says no-no to goes into the shadow. Those things that are cast out of consciousness make up your shadow, but because they're still parts of you, you need to engage, confront, and reconcile them with your shadow."

"As Prospero says about Caliban in Shakespeare's *The Tempest,* 'This thing of darkness I acknowledge mine.'"

"Yes, you've got to deal with whatever you've cast out, because in any case it will always come back in ways that will get and demand your attention."

"Jung asserted that everyone carries a shadow, and the less it is embodied in the individual's conscious life, the blacker and denser it is. And this seems to be the case for Ida."

"It *is* Ida's shadow," Klenck said, "but I think that these goblins are Sendak's shadow as well, just as the monsters in *Wild Things* and the bakers in *Night Kitchen* are his. And you could also see them as the mother's shadow."

"In an essay about *Outside Over There,* the art historian Jane Doonan wrote: 'Under the goblins' hoods, unfaced fears appear as voids.'"

"And that's why the goblin-shadow is also Ida's mother's," Klenck pointed out, "because her face is a void. The mother is a void and she's not relational—she's not relating to anybody—and so you could say that relationality itself becomes a shadow figure."

"James Baldwin," I remarked, "stated that one can only face in others what one can face in oneself, and as long as Ida flies looking up she's not going to be able to face the goblins and engage with her shadow."

"She has to turn around and confront them," Klenck told me, "and that's what her father tells her to do. Ida's all wrapped up in the mother—"

"Literally in her mother's cloak," I added.

"That's right, and it's interesting that when Ida does find the goblins, it turns out that they're actually babies with faces."

"Why do you think that the baby goblins are female and not male?" I asked her.

"Perhaps because the shadow always assumes the sex of the person whose shadow it is, so Ida's shadow is female."

"Sendak himself often suggested that Ida's anger was a consequence of her having had to take care of her baby sister," I noted, "and the goblins seem to me to represent that anger. And it's interesting that on the very last page of the book, where we see Ida now holding her baby sister with both hands, you can see that lying beneath the picket fence, where the goblins once sat, are some stones that are the same mauve-gray color as the goblins' robes."

"Yes," she said, "and this is a really wonderful way to show that Ida has finally gotten over her anger."

"There's a terrific song by Sarah McLachlan," I mentioned to Klenck, "called 'Building a Mystery,' in which she sings about a charismatic guy who lives in a church and sleeps with voodoo dolls in what she calls 'the dark side's light,' and in the song she asks him, 'Can you look out your window / Without your shadow getting in the way?'"

"What a great lyric!" Klenck exclaimed. "But it all depends on where the sun is and where your consciousness is. In *Outside Over There* Sendak has looked out the window, he's actually faced the shadow, and it's no longer distracting him. Those lines from the song would make a great motto for your book—and for Sendak as well."

"Someone," I said, "once described the shadow as 'the outside of your inside,' and it seems to me that the relationship between outside and inside is truly the heart and soul of *Outside Over There*. Sendak in fact declared that the book was like a mirror reflection, and remarked that it was called *Outside Over There* but that if you held the title up to the mirror it said *Inside In Here*."

"Yes, it's in the same vein as when the alchemists say, 'As above, so below,' or as the Jungians say, 'As outer, so inner.' Things are always reflecting each other. And what is outer and what is inner? When a fetus is in the womb, there's an inside of the baby and there's an outside of the baby, which is inside the mother's womb, and an outside of the womb, which is inside the mother. There's all this inner and outer, and we come out of that, so we're always struggling with outside over there and inside in here."

"It also seems to me," I proposed, "that the true crux and mystery of *Outside Over There* can be glimpsed in the Gnostic Gospel of Thomas, when Jesus notices some infants being suckled, and he says to his disciples, 'Those infants being suckled are like those who enter the kingdom.' And when they ask him if they too shall enter the kingdom, he replies, 'When you make the two one, when you make the inside like the outside and the outside like the inside, and the above like the below, and when you make the male and the female one and the same, then you will enter the kingdom.'"

"That's a remarkable statement," Klenck declared. "And the nursing mother with the child at her breast is the appropriate merging of the two worlds, the milk being the bridge between them."

"I'm in the milk and the milk's in me!"

"But in *Outside Over There,*" she reminded me, "the mother isn't nursing anybody, so it's Ida who has to stir up her maternal instinct . . ."

"And be a wet nurse."

"Yes. We're always struggling with outside over there and inside in here. It's a profound confusion and question: When are we being led by Self and when are we led by Other? And I think that's one of the reasons that Ida's father's voice is so disembodied, it's so outside and over there, so not in her world."

"But," I demurred, "remove the last 'e' from 'Inside In Here,' and you get 'Inside In Her.'"

"That's true, so perhaps we could say that Ida's animus is her father's voice. Her only relationship to him is *inner*. And it's as if she's carrying her father's anima."

"But doesn't the father take on the role of her daimon, her guardian spirit?"

"Yes, he's the one with the wisdom."

"So maybe we should give him a break!" I said.

"But I *do* give him a break," she replied, laughing. "Because without that father, Ida and everyone else is doomed. We're so happy when he shows up."

"When all is said and done," I said to her, "don't you think that the real key to the outside-inside mystery is Ida's window? It's her window of opportunity!"

"It is," Klenck replied, "and the window she goes through is where we get connected to life, where we're both outside and inside, above and below, up and down, mind and heart, body and soul—all those together. Yes, that window scene is astonishing."

"And with regard to that scene," I said, "there's an extraordinary poem by Rumi, as translated by Coleman Barks, that I wanted to read to you":

The breeze at dawn has secrets to tell you.

    Don't go back to sleep.

You must ask for what you really want.

    Don't go back to sleep.

People are going back and forth across the doorsill

    where the two worlds touch.

The door is round and open.

    Don't go back to sleep.

"That's exactly it," she told me, "and you should really end our conversation with this poem. And to Ida I would say, Remember what you've learned, remember what happened to you when you turned around and faced the goblins and saved your sister and recognized her, and she recognized you. Don't fall backward into your mother's depression. Stay awake. Don't go back to sleep!"

Part Six

The picture book is an art object," the art historian Jane Doonan

once declared, and over the past three decades she has lectured and

written with extraordinary insight about the aesthetics and dynamics

of children's picture books, exploring and decoding their visual gram-

mar with special regard to their lines, shapes, colors, design, pattern-

ing, viewpoint, scale, and structure, all the while never losing sight of

their cultural and psychological contexts. And she has suggested that

the prerequisites for our "getting the whole picture" are close looking,

open-mindedness, and active contemplation, since all of these allow us, in her words, "to stay put and hold on to what is being given until it has had time to work on us and we upon it."

Nowhere does Doonan better exemplify this approach than in her 1992 book *Looking at Pictures in Picture Books* and in her two-part 1986 essay entitled "*Outside Over There*: A Journey in Style," in which she looks closely at a work that she believes extends the range of how far it is possible to travel inside the covers of a picture book, but that she feels has received surprisingly little serious attention. Percy Bysshe Shelley asserted that poetry "purges from our inward sight the film of familiarity which obscures from us the wonder of our being. It compels us to feel that which we perceive, and to imagine that which we know." But it seems to me that Doonan's compelling and illuminating explorations and examinations of picture books in general, and of *Outside Over There* in particular, actually enable us to *perceive* that which we feel, and to *know* that which we have imagined.

The children's-book historian Leonard Marcus once wrote: "With *Outside Over There,* Maurice Sendak seems to have determined to create a picture book of such grandeur and virtuosity that it simply could not be ignored as art." And in order for me to get to know and perceive this book with greater clarity, I contacted Jane Doonan, who lives in Bath, England, and over a period of several days in May 2015 she and I spoke on the phone about *Outside Over There.* Acting as my docent, she took me on a fascinating visual tour of the book's Northern Romantic landscapes and parsed and elucidated for me its complex pictorial grammar.

I first asked her how she had become interested in Maurice Sendak's work.

"I was introduced to his books," she told me, "by the author and lecturer Aidan Chambers in 1983. Aidan was running a part-time children's-literature course for teachers, and one evening he turned up with a very big box full of picture books, a medium that I had taken for granted when my own children were young and in which I now had little interest. But I hadn't bargained for Aidan's powers of persuasion. He held up Sendak's *Where the Wild Things Are* and said, 'This is an example of the only literary form which uses the object itself as part of its means of communication.'"

"What did he mean by that?" I asked her.

"Aidan," she explained, "drew attention to the total design, to the shape of the book. He pointed out that its endpapers are expressive in themselves, and he talked about the double-page spread—those two opposing pages upon which the story is played out on a variety of differently shaped frames. And he also talked about the page turn, which creates a gap in the story that the viewer has to close, as well as about the text and illustrations and the relationships that are possible between them. And I have to say that my heartbeat actually changed with the excitement of discovering the picture-book medium with all its complexities. When I'd been a student of art history—I spent four happy years interrogating art objects—I was drawn to complex forms like churches carved out of caves and medieval alabaster altarpieces, which were neither paintings nor sculptures but rather painted three-dimensional objects, and now Aidan had introduced me to what has been for me the most satisfying fusion of all."

"And where did your newly awakened interest lead you next?"

"Through Aiden," she said, "I met Nancy Chambers, who was the editor of the children's-literature journal *Signal,* and Nancy published my first essay, on Anthony Browne's *Hansel and Gretel.* She also gave me an article by Kenneth Marantz entitled "The Picture Book as an Art Object: A Call for Balanced Reviewing," and in it he wrote that picture books should be perceived and valued as a form of visual art rather than literary art. So here was my written permission to call a picture book an aesthetic object. And in fact I think it likely that in all the excitement I began to try to write about picture-book makers as if they were descendants of Vermeer, and I guess that in a way I still do."

"What was it that particularly drew you to Sendak's work?"

"It was both the art and the themes he explored," she said, "but I was also deeply interested in the design—in the way, for instance, Sendak controlled rhythm by increasing the size of the frames and by withholding the text, as in *Where the Wild Things Are*. I was fascinated by how he interpreted the Grimm Brothers' tales in his book *The Juniper Tree,* which he did in a style reminiscent of etchings, and with the images filling their frames and bulging up against the picture plane as if trying to escape their destinies. And then one day Nancy Chambers passed *Outside Over There* to me, and I was enthralled, and, in the words of Baudelaire, I resolved 'to discover the why of it, and to transform my pleasure into knowledge.' "

"When you write about *Outside Over There,* as well as other picture books," I noted, "you emphasize the importance of what you call 'close looking.' "

"Yes, I call the activity of studying a picture close looking, and that involves knowing something about some basic principles of painting. If we want to be able to make the most of a picture—to be open to it and wonder why we feel as we do in front of it—we need to look not just at what's being represented but rather at everything that presents itself, and grasp at the *how* as well as the *what*. The more you know, the more you'll be able to discover and the more meanings you'll be able to make."

"You've also talked about what you call 'close looking in context,' " I said. "Could you describe that?"

"Close looking in context is obviously not the same activity as looking at a single picture. In a picture book there's almost always a text that works in a variety of relationships with the artwork to produce a composite text—the one that exists only in the reader-viewer's head. And as for the form itself, meanings are expressed through all aspects of its design. That's another source of information. So three sets of information have to be managed—that is, the picture, the words, and the book itself. Also, a picture book enables the beholder to work backward and forward at will in the process of making meaning. And for the purpose of close looking, once you take into account the text, you also have to take into account the powerful narrative thrust of the words in order to find out what happens next."

"And what would be an example of this in *Outside Over There?*"

"You can see a strong example of this tension in the first text page," she pointed out. "The narrator tells me, 'When Papa was away at sea . . .' Now there's an intriguing snippet—it's so open-ended, and I'm right away curious to know what happened *when*. Visually, there's a panorama of a shoreline and a bay with four sailing ships that are shown in the golden light of early evening. So far, so beautiful, and it's a composition that owes much to the Northern Romantic tradition as represented by painters such as Caspar David Friedrich and Philipp Otto Runge. And you can see two hooded goblins in their boat to the left of the picture plane, while on the right, Mama and Ida, who is carrying her sister, stand on the brink of the water and on the very brink of their adventure."

"Everyone except for the baby," I observed, "is looking across the water."

"Yes, the baby has her back to the scene, and through various graphic means Sendak attracts the viewer's attention to her. Although she's shown on a relatively small scale, we're drawn to her, and our narrative interest has been raised. Her face presents a round shape, which is repeated on a smaller scale by her round eyes and even smaller round nostrils—circular shapes are a means of emphasis—and her head with its saturated yellow bonnet is set

When Papa was away at sea,

against an unpatterned background of smudged gray and a tint of light blue. Also, she's located on the right side of the picture, which makes for more perceptual weight than if she were located on the left. And in this composition it's possible to believe that the story is *her* story, as Sendak has suggested it is."

"It's interesting," I mentioned, "that the mother and Ida are oblivious of the presence of the goblins."

"And apparently so too the narrator," she said. "Questions rush in. What

are these two hooded figures doing in the scene? Is Papa sailing away in the biggest of the ships? Or is he returning? Have these ships anything to do with Papa? Are the family out in the evening to enjoy the scene and think of Papa as they look at the water? Has he died? And the relationship between the words and images work together to intensify a mystery, but at the same time they don't replicate the same information, and the viewer has to make an effort to forge a connection between words and images.

"One of the richnesses of *Outside Over There,*" Doonan continued, "is the way in which the story may be interpreted literally as a heroic adventure or as a psychological journey taking place inside Ida's head, and it works perfectly either way. But the second interpretation raises an interesting question. What leads me to suppose that the goblins represent and express Ida's feelings? Sendak can't be at all sure that his reader will make that connection, but he seems to be doing his best to establish a link between goblin and girl at the very beginning of the pictorial sequence on the half-title page."

"How does he do that?"

"Well, on that page we see Ida and her little sister moving toward a hunched figure, with a black void where its face would be. The child and her charge are moving from right to left, never a strong position for a figure to hold, possibly because we read text from left to right and are comfortable with the idea that a figure heading in this direction is capable of progress, of *moving on,* whereas Ida's literally going backward across the picture plane directly in the path of trouble. On the title page Ida and the baby are hemmed

OVER THERE

MAURICE SENDAK

in by more goblins on either side, and it's as if there's no escape for the girls. Significantly, one of the goblins carries the wonder horn, which we will come to discover is Ida's emblem."

"It really surprised me," I said, "to see that wonder horn in the goblin's hands."

"It serves to link goblin and girl symbolically," Doonan explained, "and it's Sendak's strongest signal pointing toward the reading on the psychological level. The robes worn by the goblins trail behind them on the ground, leaving plenty of room for growth, whether the goblins are just babies or whether they're symbols of Ida's negative feelings about her sister."

"In fact," I noted, "it's with the power of music played on her wonder horn that Ida eventually dissolves the goblins."

"Yes, indeed, it's a victory over them, and it's also a victory over herself, which is revealed later, in the scene of reconciliation between Ida and her sister—the only episode in the story displaying pure serenity and the only occasion on which Ida and her sister gaze at each other. And it's an interesting thought that on the symbolic level Ida and the goblins are one, and that perhaps she herself poses the greatest danger of all for the baby, since she's not ready to take on the role of caring for her when the story opens."

"Could you provide another example of close looking in context?"

"One of the contexts in which picture books are used is in the classroom," Doonan informed me, "and I want to tell you about some close looking done by thirteen-year-old Bethany, working independently during a twenty-hour teaching program that I ran for young adolescents in a secondary school. The aim was to give students insights, new ideas, to bring to pictures—to move adolescents beyond the point where their organizing insight only had to do with expressiveness. But I should mention that they were already familiar with the concept of themes, and had some understanding of how a writer creates effects through style and literary devices."

"So how did this work?"

"The class was given a free choice from a box of forty picture books, which included several by Sendak," Doonan explained to me, "and Bethany selected *Outside Over There*. She comes from a large and musical family, which may go some way to explaining why she chose this Sendak book, and she wrote: 'The small details which aroused my interest so much portray images strongly linked to Mozart, who is shown sitting in his summer cottage in a garden in Vienna in the summer of 1791. And the three figures standing on the small brick-arched bridge seem to suggest to me a resemblance to the three boys who are the slaves of Monostatos the Moor in Mozart's *The Magic Flute.*'"

"I'd completely overlooked that," I said, "even though it was actually hiding in plain sight."

"I'd overlooked that too," Doonan admitted, "and although what we perceive is dependent on our prior experiences, it nevertheless takes a very sharp eye to spot those boys, and it requires a searching attitude to suggest whom they might represent. And although she wanted a happy ending, Bethany also thought that all was not going to be well forever for the sisters. She based her opinion on the tonal differences among, as she stated them, the soft pastel shades of the sky, the composer, the main characters, the darkness of the near woods and riverbank, and the tree with branches outstretched like, as Bethany stated it, 'claws ready to grasp.'"

I mentioned to Doonan that William Blake often referred to what he called "minute particulars." Blake thought that every word and every letter in a poem should be studied, and that every line and every stroke in a painting should be similarly paid attention to, and declared, "He who wishes to see

Now Ida glad hugged baby tight and she followed the

a Vision, a perfect Whole, must see it in its Minute Particulars, Organized."
In *Outside Over There* Sendak exhibits a wonderful solicitude for minute particulars, and I asked Doonan if she could point to some of the ones that she found particularly compelling.

"First of all," Doonan replied, "there are minute particulars of objects that have a function in the visual narrative, and then there are also the minute particulars with regard to the style Sendak adopts to create a world for Ida that's both intensely real and surreal."

"And what would be an example of the former?"

"Well, if you look at the dedication page, you can, for example, see Ida

stream that curled like a path along the broad meadow

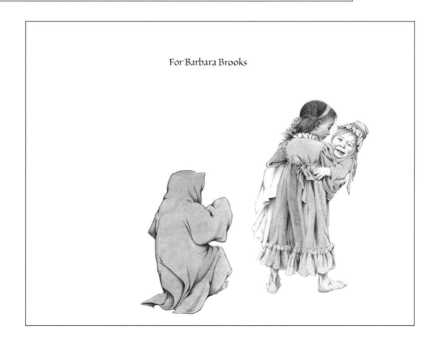

For Barbara Brooks

from behind carrying the baby while a goblin creeps toward the girls. The bow of Ida's sash is in disarray, and this is such a telling little detail, since it hints at the weight of the struggling baby as she pulls on Ida's clothes, but of course it's also a metaphor for Ida's feelings, which are also disarrayed.

Or, to take another example, look at the ribbon of the baby's bonnet, which is first shown on the half-title page, where you see Ida encouraging the baby to take her first steps. The baby's carrying the bonnet by its ribbon ties, and then in the book's final image we see the bonnet still dangling by its ties from her hand, and the repetition of this minute particular supports the interpretation that what happens in *Outside Over There* is indeed taking place in Ida's head, in the time needed for the baby to make a step. So what Sendak's suggesting here is an extraordinary compression of time."

"And what," I asked her, "would be some examples of the minute particulars with regard to style?"

"Just observe the way Sendak enlists the dramatic power of lighting effects. For instance, dark cumulus clouds are rimmed brightly by reflected light from the moon. Light also creates the almost metallic gleam on Ida's yellow rain cloak's slick surfaces, and it polishes the wooden frame of the arbor and touches upon strands of Ida's sister's fine baby hair broken by a tiny ear."

"That's absolutely beautiful!" I exclaimed.

"And flickers of light," Doonan added, "prompt our memories and suggest to us exactly how it might feel to stand barefoot on the dense moss-green grass in Mama's arbor."

"Sendak," I mentioned, "once asserted that for him, style was purely a means to an end, that the more styles you had, the better, and he talked about having a fine style, a fat style, a fairly slim style, and an extremely stout style. So I wonder if you could say something about the three different styles of the books that comprise his trilogy—*Where the Wild Things Are, In the Night*

Kitchen, and *Outside Over There*—since these three books really seem to me to exemplify Sendak's extraordinary stylistic flexibility."

"Take *Wild Things,*" said Doonan. "Sendak illustrates that book in pen-and-ink line and watercolor in a style that combines graphic and painterly effects, and the picture plane seethes with controlled energy as he uses a multitude of marks over the washes of paint. Hatching and cross-hatching model the figures and their settings and settle the images on the page, and this linear technique, which has its origins in etching and engraving, gives his pictures a traditional resonance."

"And the artwork," I observed, "has an almost tactile quality."

"And you can almost feel the fur, feathers, and scales that differentiate one wild thing from another," she added. "The grass springs underfoot, and the waves surge and splash, and forms are lost and found against densely patterned foliage. And as for color, delicate tints contrast with richer, more muted tones. Sendak's on record as saying that at the time that he created *Wild Things* he didn't want to use fat, bright colors."

"But he of course used them in *Night Kitchen,*" I said.

"Yes, for that book he brought out those bright colors as he celebrates Mickey's nocturnal adventures in comics-art form. And all of its conventions are there—panels carrying the frames, text boxes, speech balloons, text treated graphically with the size of lettering increasing to imply high levels in volume of sound, and there are also printed labels or signs on pictured objects. The color's rich and it's held in a black, sensuous, and infinitely varying line. And as for the images themselves, at dramatic moments in the plot they inflate before our very eyes. The early twentieth-century cartoonist Winsor McCay is a major influence on his style, and so too the popular art of Sendak's childhood, including such figures as Mickey Mouse and King Kong."

"And what about *Outside Over There,* which seems so stylistically different from the other two books?"

"In 1971," Doonan reminded me, "in preparation for illustrating a selection of tales by the Brothers Grimm, Sendak visited Germany to absorb the language, the landscape, and the atmosphere, and he found everything he needed there. In fact, Sendak stated that one of those Grimms' tales, 'The Goblins,' was the main literary source for *Outside Over There.*"

"Sendak," I said, "noted that *Outside Over There* was also his tribute to Mozart, and he thought of the book as a kind of symbolic portrait of the composer."

"It's interesting," Doonan pointed out, "that to complement the Grimm country and to match the historical period of Mozart's life, he adopted the painterly style of the Northern Romantic artists of the late eighteenth century. And that style gives historical unity to Ida's story and provides its emotional charge as well as its visual vocabulary and iconography. Sendak wants us to feel that we're witnessing or empathizing with an immense journey and a spiritual experience."

"Where did that tradition come from?"

"The roots of Romanticism are various," she informed me, "but it was in Germany that the movement first emerged. Caspar David Friedrich and Philipp Otto Runge were two of the greatest early Romantic painters, and *Outside Over There* might be seen as an homage to both of them. As the art scholar Robert Rosenblum has pointed out, Friedrich is the first of the painters whose canvases transpose the experience of the supernatural from traditional religious imagery to nature, and one of his recurring compositional motifs was that of figures whom we see from the back, standing both literally and figuratively on the brink of some mystical experience in nature as they gaze into the moonrise or sunset. And the first double-page spread in *Outside*

Caspar David Friedrich: *The Stages of Life* (1835)

Over There—'When Papa was away at sea,' which we talked about before—replicates the Romantic mood and its symmetrical composition."

"What are some of the typical motifs of this tradition?"

"Trees, flowers, ships, and the moon were some of the favored ones, and they were all adopted by Sendak for *Outside Over There*. Friedrich portrayed individual trees as if they had almost human presence, and the sunflower, which is a major presence in Sendak's book, had previously been used by painters such as Blake, Runge, and Van Gogh to suggest various spiritual conditions. And a chorus of sunflowers accompanies Ida on the earlier stages of her adventure, as does the moon, which is a mysterious and powerful pagan deity that has been an enduring and recurring motif in Sendak's work. Ships in moonlight were another favorite Romantic image, and he shows Papa's ship sailing on the moon-shimmering waves that run beyond the goblin caves."

"For me," I confessed, "the most emotionally overwhelming moment in

Outside Over There occurs in the recognition scene, where for the first time in the book Ida finally looks at her baby sister, who's just emerged reborn from her eggshell, face to face, as Ida raises her hands in a gesture of benediction. What is it about this scene that makes it so affecting?"

"First of all, on the literal and secular level of the story it's a relief to see that the baby's safe, and the two sisters are together and exchanging gazes and gestures of delight in each other. That's affecting in itself, and any young viewer will feel it to be so from the naturalism with which Sendak portrays the siblings. Ida's expression is tender, the baby's flesh is almost palpable, and at the same time he captures the atmosphere of a religious painting by association."

"And how does he do that?"

"Notice the setting," she said, "which is at the mouth of a cave beside a

stream. We see rocky formations and a gauzy luminous cloudscape framing the figures of the sisters, and I should mention that strange rocks that create a grotto setting are a common feature in Leonardo's work—just think of *The Virgin of the Rocks.* And then there's the exchange of gestures with the baby's pointing forefinger. There are multitudes of pointing angels on wood and walls in museums, churches, and palaces, and we have a sublime example from Michelangelo on the ceiling of the Sistine Chapel as God reaches out to give life to Adam."

"Also, the color of Ida's dress is Marian blue," I observed.

"Ida's in her blue dress kneeling in front of her sister, and as she looks down on her, she raises her hands as if in wonder. And we can say that she's a secular version of the Virgins of the Flemish, German, and Italian Renaissance, whose newborn infants lie before them in cribs or mandorlas of light. The figure of Mary in this pose probably has its origins in the vision of Saint Bridget of Sweden and can be found in countless nativity paintings. As for the blue dress, sometime during the thirteenth century ultramarine arrived in Italy as the most expensive pigment on the market, so its use was restricted to color the Virgin's robes as a mark of her precious worth."

"And then there's Ida's sister," I said. "The holy child."

"Yes, we see Ida's newly hatched baby sister sitting in a broken eggshell," Doonan pointed out, "which on a literal level serves as a cradle, and this is possible because Sendak has destroyed the natural relationship of scale between a human baby and an egg in the cause of supernatural reality. The child–chick's eggshell expresses the ideas of rebirth and renewal, and a mysterious light source unifies the various elements and enhances the otherworldly effect. And I think that of all the paintings in the *Outside Over There* sequence, this one gets closest to the Northern Romantic yearning to find the sacred in the secular."

"In *Outside Over There*," I mentioned, "Sendak presents two of his most dramatic and brilliantly realized visual sequences, and I was wondering if you could describe and say something about them. The first of these depicts Ida's response to the kidnapping of her baby sister."

"Among the ways in which Sendak creates those dramatic effects," she told me, "is changes of scale within the pictures, such that, for example, the farther away a form appears to be, the more detached we're likely to feel,

Ida played her wonder horn
to rock the baby still –
but never watched.

whereas the nearer the form, the more closely involved we become. And in this first sequence, Sendak's going to bring Ida increasingly close to us."

"How does he do that?"

"Well, it begins in the interior of a small parlor with two windows. On the back wall and reflected in a mirror we see a portrait, presumably of Ida's sailor papa, but he also, come to think of it, looks a little bit like Philipp Otto Runge. Ida's standing in front of the window to the left and is playing

So the goblins came.
They pushed their way in
and pulled baby out,
leaving another all made of ice.

Poor Ida, never knowing, hugged the changeling
and she murmured: "How I love you."

The ice thing only dripped and stared,
and Ida mad knew goblins had been there.

"They stole my sister away!" she cried,
"To be a nasty goblin's bride!"
 Now Ida in a hurry

snatched her Mama's yellow rain cloak,
tucked her horn safe in a pocket,
and made a serious mistake.

her wonder horn, while two goblins prepare to enter the room through the central window on their ladder. The baby's looking helplessly at Ida, and then in the next frame she's abducted by the goblins, who leave an ice baby in her place."

"And the sky that we see through the window," I said, "has turned ominously dark."

"Yes and now Sendak makes some dramatic changes. The next four frames show a section of the room at a child's eye level, which inevitably causes Papa's portrait to disappear, and Sendak moves the forms closer together through changes of scale. He distorts the perspective and further darkens the sky outside, and then changes the proportions of the second window, which has now lost its glazing bars and thus begins to function like a screen and carries an additional visual narrative that's occurring simultaneously to the main story."

"And on that screen," I noticed, "we can see a square-rigger sailing in heavy seas, and the next view of it, on the opposing frame, shows the ship foundering."

"So could this be Papa's story?" Doonan wondered. "Though let's hope not. But there are increasing numbers of aggressive-looking, pointed-petal sunflowers invading the room, as if to echo Ida's rising rage at the goblins' trick."

"Now Ida dramatically takes on the role of a warrior," I said, "which is such a powerful image."

"It is, and the sequence moves to its conclusion. Over the next two page frames we witness the equivalent of the vow and ritual-arming of a young knight. Ida's positioned on the center of the picture plane on a large scale and in profile, with her arms raised, her fists clenched, and her form creates a powerful rising diagonal. And the sea outside is momentarily calmed."

"And then in the opposing frame Ida dons her mother's golden raincoat—"

"—and she grasps her wonder horn," Doonan continued, "and prepares herself for her quest. And the heavy clouds and the high seas that we see through the central window frame symbolically prefigure the trial that's awaiting her."

"And that trial," I said, "is depicted in the four astonishing scenes in which we see her confronting the goblins and churning them, in the words of Sendak's text, into a dancing stream."

"Yes, and all these scenes are displayed in double-page frames, which create a landscape format and allow for maximum breadth of picture space, which is an appropriate metaphor for the low cave system in which the next episode takes place. And Sendak in fact narrows the available depth for his paintings by running his text on a generous white border along the lower edge of each page."

"In the text," I mentioned, "he describes the following four scenes as a hubbub, which I've always thought of as a kind of parallel to the three rumpus scenes in *Where the Wild Things Are.*"

"And in the first picture of this hubbub," Doonan pointed out, "Ida, who's on the left, crawls on all fours into a cavern and arrives just in time to see a group of tumbling, nude, crotchety babies holding a wedding. A sublime cloudscape in hues of rose madder, light ocher, and gray forms an iridescent backdrop for the scene. The composition, which is based on a repetition of large and small triangular shapes, displays an elegant symmetry."

"Ida totally dominates the following double-page frame, doesn't she?"

"She does, and Ida, who fills the available space to the left with her cloak spreading around her, is down on one knee playing her horn while the goblins, who are swept away by her music, are prancing along the cavern

So Ida tumbled right side round and found herself
smack in the middle of a wedding.

Oh, how those goblins hollered and kicked,
just babies like her sister!

"What a hubbub," said Ida sly,
and she charmed them with a captivating tune.

The goblins, all against their will, danced slowly first,
then faster until they couldn't breathe.

"Terrible Ida," the goblins said,
"we're dancing sick and must to bed."

But Ida played a frenzied jig, a hornpipe
that makes sailors wild beneath the ocean moon.

Those goblins pranced so fierce, so fast,

they quick churned into a dancing stream.

floor. The walls are opening out, and color and light are pouring in. And then, when you turn the page, Ida's position has changed dramatically—now we see her leaping in front of the goblins, playing a frenzied jig, and the cloak that's streaming from her outstretched hand entangles them in a torrent of fabric. And the moon, as witness, appears huge in the sky in Northern Romantic style."

"Next comes that amazing dissolution scene."

"Yes, the final frame of this sequence shows Ida, wonder horn in hand, in a scale so large that she has to bend over double in her confined setting, while the goblins behind her are fast transforming into a stream. Their finely modeled faces and actions are still full of life, but their bulging baby flesh is dissolving."

"What an incredibly haunting and mysterious moment this is," I exclaimed.

"It is, and Sendak achieves that mysterious effect through minute dabbings, blottings, flurries, and layerings of semitransparent paint in low-key color, together with delicate trails of foaming white. Now you see the form, now you don't. The quest's over, and this is Ida's moment of victory over herself and the goblins."

"Ida triumphant!" I declared.

"That's right, and you see her flourishing the golden cloak, which now acts as a barrier to close off any further influence from those malignant spirits."

"But to me," I confessed, "the most astonishing illustration in *Outside Over There* is the double-page dreamscape that shows Ida floating way up high on a cloud, and I think that it's one of Sendak's most extraordinary and complex creations. You once wrote that Sendak invites us to 'travel the picture,' just as Ida floats and travels. How does he allow us to do that in this particular scene?"

"This picture aims at creating both large and small movements," Doonan explained, "and Sendak is relying upon the beholder's share to set them in motion. So let's start with the white rectangular label which carries the text of Papa's song ["If Ida backwards in the rain / would only turn around again / and catch those goblins with a tune / she'd spoil their kidnap honeymoon"], and this device enables Sendak to extend his picture to the very edges of all four sides of the double-page spread, because no bordering of any kind is needed to carry the text. So in effect he's giving us an unbounded fragment of Ida's world to explore."

"And there's a lot to explore," I said.

"There's plenty to see," she agreed, "including a tall sailing ship, a ruined church, a sleeping shepherd and his flock. We also find images of a pair of sailors, the baby, a pair of goblins, a lamp, and Mama, and each is set as an isolated unit along the lower foreground. And these small pictures within the main one show simultaneously what's happening outside over there to all the participants on the literal level . . . or perhaps the whole scene might be interpreted as Ida's reverie, or as the journey of her soul."

"It's also amazing how brilliantly Sendak makes use of multiple viewpoints."

"And rather than giving us a fixed viewpoint," she said, "he employs multiple eye levels, directing our attention in a way that corresponds to an upward or downward movement of the head. More than one eye level frees the viewer to travel the picture plane."

"How can we do this?"

"For example, we rise to look into Ida's eyes and read her expression. We drop down to the water's edge to meet the sailors' enigmatic gazes. We need to stoop to get close to the baby in her glowing cave, and stoop even more to examine the mysterious lamp that's shedding a cold light on the

walls of its niche. From afar, we observe sad Mama, a small figure, still sitting in her arbor. And a low viewpoint obliges us to look up to the goblins that guard the baby. So it's worth remembering that a viewpoint is also a point of view, and in this double-page spread Sendak's contriving the degree to which we enter the painting or remain detached spectators, as well as allowing us to move in space and to live the image."

"You've written extensively and have thought a lot about *Outside Over*

"If Ida backwards in the rain
would only turn around again
and catch those goblins with a tune
she'd spoil their kidnap honeymoon!"

There over the years," I said to Doonan, "and I'm wondering if you might be able to sum up your thoughts about this amazing book."

"Let me do so," she replied, "by borrowing some words from Caspar David Friedrich, who said that the artist should paint not only what he sees *before* him but also what he sees *within* him. And I think this is what Sendak did when he created Ida and her world."

Part Seven

I've been Maurice Sendak's devoted fan since I was four years old,"

the playwright and screenwriter Tony Kushner once remarked, "and

my admiration for him has not only grown in adulthood, but he's also

been an important influence on my own work." The author of many

plays, including *Angels in America,* as well as the filmscript for Steven

Spielberg's *Lincoln,* Kushner was a close friend of Sendak's for nearly

twenty years. His illuminating biography, *The Art of Maurice Sendak:*

1980 to the Present, was published in 2003; and that same year he also

wrote the text for a remarkable picture book, illustrated by Sendak, that was based on the 1938 children's opera *Brundibár,* by the Jewish Czech composer Hans Krása, which was performed fifty-five times by the children of Theresiestadt, a Nazi concentration camp. In the opera a little brother and sister decide to sing in the town square in order to raise money to buy some milk for their sick mother but are hindered by the malevolent hurdy-gurdy grinder Brundibár, who is finally kicked out of town with the assistance of a sparrow, a cat, a dog, and a posse of local schoolkids. And in 2005 the Sendak-Kushner book, which one critic described as a "heartbreaking, hopeful masterpiece," was turned into an acclaimed operatic production with sets and costumes designed by Sendak and a new English libretto written by Kushner.

In June 2015, Tony Kushner and I met at an Upper West Side restaurant for a lengthy breakfast, over which he reminisced about his friendship with Sendak. "I'm doing this interview with you," Kushner said to me, "not only for your book but also for me, because I miss Maurice terribly." We talked for several hours about his friend's extraordinary life and work and about the role that *Outside Over There* played in them.

I began our conversation by asking him how he came to meet Sendak.

"In 1993, *Angels in America* was coming to Broadway," he told me, "and at that time I gave an interview to *The New York Times* in which I mentioned that Herman Melville was my favorite American author. It turned out that he was Maurice's favorite American author as well, and Maurice asked a mutual friend of ours if he could introduce us, which he did. But you could really say that Maurice and I actually met because of Herman. And we became friends immediately. I drove up to Connecticut to see his incredible Melville book collection, which included signed and inscribed first editions of many of Melville's books, and after that I visited him once or twice a month and brought him groceries and food."

"Hot pastrami with coleslaw and mustard on rye was what he requested from me," I mentioned.

"Yes," Kushner confirmed, "that's what one did." He laughed. "And presents too."

"Do you recall how and when you first discovered Sendak's books?"

"I was brought up in Louisiana," Kushner said, "and a cousin of mine had copies of Sesyle Joslin's *What Do You Say, Dear?* and Ruth Krauss's *A Hole Is To Dig,* both of which Maurice had illustrated, and I remember devouring those books and loving them, and I can still remember what was on every single page. And then when I was about five or six there was a woman named Rosa Hart who was a kind of culture doyenne in Lake Charles—I remember that she smoked like a chimney—and she had a little bookstore under a staircase in a big department store, and it was called The Three R's. It was mostly a children's bookstore, and either Rosa gave me as a present or my mother or grandmother bought for me the *Nutshell Library,* four tiny books from a tiny bookstore, and I thought it was the greatest thing I'd ever seen. It was four fantastic books and a toy at the same time, and I remember looking at all the details, like the little frames Maurice drew around the outside of the box with its corner faces. And for a kid, you could tell that they were made for you, they were just the right size."

"Which of the four books do you remember especially liking?"

"Well, *Pierre* and *Chicken Soup with Rice* were of course incredible. But I wasn't the only one to think so. Maurice once told me that the poet Marianne Moore, who, like him, had lived on West Ninth Street in Greenwich Village, once confided to him that *Chicken Soup with Rice* was a poem that she would have loved to have written."

"There's something unique and truly inimitable about the kids in a lot of those early Sendak books, don't you think?"

"Absolutely, it's the way Maurice had of showing their incredible self-involvement and tyrannical will and vulnerability, but also the incredible strength of character that kids sometimes have, which can sometimes be a slightly unpleasant strength of character. And have you ever noticed that little children don't amble or saunter? They goose-step! And I thought that Sendak's kids kind of looked like Mussolini."

"Like Mussolini?"

"Yes," Kushner replied, laughing, "and only Maurice noticed that. To me, his top-heavy and heavy-footed immigrant-looking kids are sort of preposterous and laughable and somehow also predictive of a kind of adult egoism, yet they're also enormously sympathetic. And right from the beginning with Maurice there's a very deep understanding of children that isn't in any way sentimentalized or cute, and I always responded to that."

"Did you also know about *The Sign on Rosie's Door* in those days?"

"I did, and I've always thought of Rosie as a kind of prototype of a children's-book author."

"In what sense?" I asked him.

"In the sense that she enlisted and organized all the other neighborhood kids into an imaginary world that she created. She was Prospero, and she would say, I'm going to make a play out of you, and here are the terms of the universe that you're going to live in for the length of this play. She was this big, bossy girl with a loud voice and a penchant for dressing up and being continually surprising and shocking. And the other kids just surrendered and went with her. She was the field marshal; she decided what the rules of the world were going to be. And I think that for Maurice she was the prototype of the artist."

"I've discussed Sendak's visual style with the English art historian Jane Doonan," I mentioned to Kushner, "but since Sendak once declared that for him, illustrating meant having 'a passionate affair with words,' I'd like to ask you about his idiosyncratic prose style, with what you've called its 'bumps in the road' and its blending of 'the elegant and the inelegant, and the polished and crude.'"

"The person who really taught Maurice how to write for kids was Ruth Krauss," Kushner told me. "She was a poet and a playwright and was influenced by jazz, which I don't think was a music that ever had any serious meaning for Maurice, but it provided her writing with an improvisational freedom, and gave her this permission to make any noise on paper that you'd want to make, to write 'boobly-boobly-boobly-doo' and things that sounded like kids' speech, and it was also like scat singing, veering from very long,

This is the last picture of any kind Maurice Sendak worked on. It was left unfinished on his drawing table when he was hospitalized in May 2012. The woman wearing a Rosie-like hat is a character in his story tentatively titled *No Nose*. The picture is published here for the first time.

elegant lines to very syncopated, short and choppy, and conversational ones. I think that Ruth's style planted itself deeply in Maurice and helped give him a voice, but then he took it to a place that Ruth didn't. He learned how to turn off the censors and free-associate, and if an impulse came in, he was extraordinarily brave about welcoming it and letting it sit around for a while and seeing what it had to say to him."

"Sendak," I said, "described the language in *Where the Wild Things Are* as being 'very erectile—ba-*room,* ba-*room*—it just pushes forward and then peters out, literally,' while the language in *Outside Over There,* he noted, was 'very perverse and going its own strange route.'"

"When I was working on the text for *Brundibar,*" Kushner recalled, "I originally wrote a rhymed verse narrative and showed it to Maurice, and he said, Oh, it's wonderful, but I could tell that he really didn't like it. And then Maurice's editor, Michael di Capua, also read what I'd written, and he said, 'It's relentless, it's unusable, you feel like somebody's driving nails into your head,' and he was right. So I sat down and thought and wondered how I was going to do this, and what I finally did was basically just rip off Maurice's style, that business of switching around syntax and putting the adjectives in the wrong place."

"Sendak," I said, "asserted that the entire construction of the book gives the sense of being written backward."

"Could you remind me of some of the backward phrases in *Outside Over There*?" Kushner asked me.

"Here's one of them: 'The ice thing only dripped and stared, and Ida mad knew goblins had been there.' And another one is: 'Those goblins pranced so fierce, so fast, they quick churned into a dancing stream.' In a sense you could say that the language goes backward, just as Ida floats backward out her window."

"Yes, that's beautiful," Kushner responded. "But to me it also feels like immigrant speech, and it sounds like some of the old Yiddish-language poets who tried timidly to write in English. In my biography of Maurice I say that he made use of certain features of that speech in his books: the deliberate so-called errors of syntax, the way language flows over its own mistakes, and flows *because* of its mistakes. In a way it's like what the critic Helen Vendler has pointed out: you look for a place in the line where there isn't normal speech, where it seems to be invented, and it's exactly there that the meaning and the poetry are. That's where the iron will of language is broken a little, and it therefore gets freed up to say things that it can't actually say directly. And in *Outside Over There* you can sense Maurice's sensitivity to that."

"I know that Sendak loved to read poetry, especially poems by Emily Dickinson and John Keats."

"Maurice had an incredible love of poetry," Kushner told me, "and when I'd visit him in Connecticut I'd recite poems to him, and he'd always look at me with an expression that was something between horror and awe, because he had a poor memory for stuff like that. He couldn't believe that I could remember all those lines, and I could make him cry if I recited ten lines of Keats. Beautiful language completely transported him."

"He once wrote that he loved 'immaculate, rigid, antiquated forms where every bit of fat is cut off, so tight and perfect you couldn't stick a pin in it, but within which you can be as free as you want,'" I said. "And when I read that, I immediately thought of Hamlet when he proclaims, 'O God, I could be bounded in a nutshell and count myself a king of infinite space were it not that I have bad dreams.' And of course I also thought of the *Nutshell Library*."

"It's interesting that you quoted that line to me, because I included it in the film *Lincoln* when he recounts a disturbing dream that he's had to his wife. But on the other hand I think that there's also a part of Maurice's work that's enormously opulent and voluptuous. He perfected very intricate cross-hatching in *Higglety Pigglety Pop!,* just as he did in *The Juniper Tree* and in his illustrations for Randall Jarrell's *The Bat-Poet* and *The Animal Family,* but he drops it completely when he goes into the Brooklyn poster-art, comic-book world of *In the Night Kitchen.* You don't see a Matisse-like winnowing down to distilled essence—Maurice is willing to get very big and silly as well as very spare, depending on the subject matter. So there's very spare Sendak but also very voluptuous Sendak. There's the German romanticism of the landscapes in *Outside Over There,* but just look at Ida when she's wrapped in her mother's voluptuous yellow cloak. She's got this huge body and feet and seems to be going through a kind of adolescence as she floats upside down on her cloud. I mean, it's Bernini's *Ecstasy of Saint Teresa.* Maurice could never resist drapery, and this is a Baroque image, and Maurice loved that."

"I suppose I'm sounding a bit intransigent when I insist on emphasizing Sendak's love for the art of condensation," I admitted.

"I guess what I'm reacting to with regard to that notion of rigid forms," Kushner explained, "is that all great artists aspire to pare away and make everything essential and make everything count, but that sort of Beckettian idea of boring down to the smallest thing and stripping everything away isn't all there is in Maurice's work. I can understand why he admired people who attained a maximum meaning with a minimum of means, but there's an effusiveness in Maurice's imagination that's slightly at odds with that classical ideal, and I think he never lost his appetite for the superabundant and excessive. All the way to the end, his work stays so sensual and full of life."

"Sendak once said to you, 'I must learn to unlearn appetite,' but he apparently never succeeded in doing that."

"No, he really didn't," Kushner acknowledged. "I have to tell you that shortly after Gene [Eugene Glynn] died, in 2007, Maurice began to suffer from really extreme back pain, and he began to adopt the Buddhist attitude of 'I'm no longer going to hate everybody.' I remember that one day we went for a long walk, and he seemed very happy and at peace with himself after all that suffering and torment. And I said, 'You seem really great,' and he told me, 'I really think I've let it go'—at that moment he was working on what would be his last published work, *My Brother's Book*—and he added, 'I don't care if the book never gets published. I don't have any more ambitions, I don't need to collect anymore, I don't need to buy things, I don't get envious now when I hear that someone's published a new book—suddenly it doesn't bother me. I'm just happy to be alive.' And then this car pulls up and the window goes down, and it's one of his neighbors, who says, 'Maurice, I was watching the *American Masters* film about Jim Henson on TV last night, it was all about him and the Muppets, and it made me think of you. You're *just* like Jim Henson, you're one of our national treasures!' And Maurice turned to me and snarled, 'That fucking Jim Henson, he *stole* from me!' So, so much for that!" He laughed.

"There's an old saying," I said to Kushner, "that goes 'Not to be confined by the greatest, but to be contained within the smallest, is divine.' And Sendak once told Bill Moyers that because he didn't have much confidence in himself when he was young, he decided, as he put it, to 'hide inside this modest form called a children's book and express myself entirely. I wasn't going to paint or do ostentatious drawings or gallery pictures, I would just hide somewhere where nobody would ever find me.'"

"It's all true except for the last thing," Kushner remarked, "because Maurice in fact hid himself so *little*. Now of course it is completely true that instead of going into the 1950s art world and contending with monster people like Jackson Pollock and all the stuff that was happening then, he went into a form where he thought he could hide. And he hides in it, but he then turns himself completely inside out and shows everybody everything."

"In a sense," I suggested, "it's a bit like what happens when an actor puts on a mask. As the director Peter Brook once observed, the fact that the mask gives you something to hide behind makes it unnecessary for you to hide. And because there is security you can take greater risks, and because everything about you is hidden, you can therefore let yourself appear. So don't you think that in this sense one could say that the picture book was Maurice's mask?"

"Yes," said Kushner, "it's like the contract you make when you dream, because you're safe, recumbent, and immobile, and you can therefore allow yourself to see things and stage little plays in your dream that will tell you unbearable things, but if you accessed that at every waking moment, you'd become incoherent and incapable of moving. And similarly, as Peter Brook said, in acting you're in a safe place, so you can put yourself at immense risk and enter into great danger. And this danger, as Shakespeare would say, is not real, but it's also very real at the same time, though it's not what we conventionally mean by real. As Hippolyta tells Theseus in *A Midsummer Night's Dream,* it's 'all the story of the night told over, / And all their minds transfigured so together.' And in this case there's Maurice Sendak, kiddie-book writer, but also this great artist daring to say and do and dream outrageous, painful, difficult things. So yes, it's revealing through hiding."

"The psychoanalyst D. W. Winnicott once remarked that 'it is a joy to be hidden, and a disaster not to be found.'"

"That's a beautiful statement," Kushner said, "and in a sense that's what *Outside Over There* is about. The book is a very high-stakes Easter egg hunt—although Maurice wouldn't have liked the goyishe image—so maybe we should instead say the search for the *afikoman* [the broken piece of matzo often hidden by parents for the children to find after the Passover seder]. But Ida too is looking for something—it's her baby sister—and it's a game of hide-and-seek, but this one is for absolutely terrifying stakes. Or it's like that story about Maurice's sister, Natalie, losing him at the World's Fair—it's both a life-and-death struggle and a game at the same time.

"I think that *Outside Over There* is very much about Ida's ambivalence, because she's stuck in a caregiving role, and any little girl taking care of a baby sibling knows that at some point she may eventually have a child of her own, and that the child will diminish her in some ways—as well as enrich her—but she'll have to limit her own independent life by concentrating on being the mother to her child. And that sort of letting go of the hand and hoping the kid is going to step out on her own—"

"It may have been a mistake to have let the baby's hand go so soon," I interjected.

"But it's a necessary mistake," Kushner said. "There's so much danger in just getting that massive head up on two legs as a secure thing. You've got the brain up there, and you're going to fall over a hundred million times before you can master just being upright. It's a dangerous thing to do, but it's a necessary one, and it's a kind of freedom for the mother as well as the child. Helping a kid to reach childhood is a combination of incredible skill, of knowing the rite, knowing the steps—when do you hold the hand and when do you let it go—and it requires luck and improvisation, and it's miraculous that any of us make it."

"Sendak," I said, "thought of the picture book as his battleground, and he stated that it was there that he fought his battles and hoped to win his wars."

"I think Maurice certainly wins the war in *Outside Over There,*" Kushner replied, "and to me it's his last completely successful great book."

"But Sendak almost didn't win the battle," I noted. "He once explained that *Where the Wild Things Are* was what he called 'excavation work,' and he compared what he was doing to what Herman Melville called 'diving.' Sendak insisted that you needed to dive deep and then you either came up or you drowned, but you either took the risk or you sold out."

"That somebody who writes children's books dares to talk of himself in those terms is thrilling," Kushner declared. "And remember, he's talking about producing books for kids and yet he's absolutely refusing to sound like somebody who's making little decals to hang up in a nursery. He's talking about the struggle and pain of producing a great work of art, and anybody who knew Maurice knew that it was true. There's no cultural permission to be Maurice Sendak, and as the poet Paul Valéry said, anybody who's a genius and doesn't know it probably isn't one. And that's Maurice—he knew it."

"It's interesting that when he's talking about his struggle he refers to Melville's idea of diving."

"It's the Melvillian depths," said Kushner, "and I think that Maurice felt very afraid of how far he had gone in *Outside Over There*. You know, there's a letter that Melville wrote to Evert Duyckinck in which he talked about 'thought-divers' who dive down and come back up again with bloodshot eyes and perhaps with a pearl in their hands, and he declared that it was 'better to sink in boundless deeps than float on vulgar shoals.' And in Melville's novel *Mardi* there's an amazing scene when they're in the lagoon and suddenly this enormous wave comes and pushes them out of the lagoon, and he said that it was at that very moment that he thought, I could spend the rest of my life writing nineteenth-century sea novels, but I can also give permission to this insanely great soul inside of me to burst forth. And he does, and he starts the move toward *Moby-Dick*. And in doing so he had to take a risk. As he says in *Mardi,* 'Give me, ye Gods, an utter wreck, if wreck I do.'"

"In *Outside Over There*," I noted, "Ida likewise takes a risk when she decides to go out her window in order to rescue her sister from the goblins. But at first she botches it, because she floats out backward and upside down."

"It's like Melville saying, 'All my books are botches,' " Kushner reminded me. "But in fact the creative process *is* the willingness to make terrible mistakes, to blunder, just as Ida makes a mistake when she lets go of her baby sister's hand. You quoted Maurice saying that when he was beginning to write *Outside Over There* his unconscious would spit up a word and then say, Look at this schmuck just sitting around, give him another word or else he'll just sit there forever. And it's that clumsy, bungling thing you do when you start out on a creative endeavor—you don't know what the fuck you're doing, and then slowly, once you've got the wonder horn and the tools you need, things begin to happen."

"So you're saying that the mistake can be the catalyst?"

"Yes, the mistake is always where you begin. You begin by putting yourself at risk, by doing something wrong, by transgressing."

"Like Melville," I suggested, "Sendak also dove into uncharted psychological waters, and as you pointed out in your Sendak biography, he was one of the first children's-book authors to recognize the fact of children's sexual curiosity, and was one of the first to push at this boundary. Sendak in fact once said to me, 'People objected to Mickey bathing in milk and floating naked—every part of his body having a sensuous experience, as if that's naughty. Why? Why are we all so screwed up, including me? But at least creatively I try to convey the memory of a time in life when it was a pleasure.' "

"Exactly," said Kushner. "Why are we so messed up? But Maurice himself was a fairly anxious person, he didn't really live it, and he believed that there were certain strictures that you needed to place on human interaction in order to form a coherent culture. And in fact in Maurice's books he's profoundly respectful of latency. As I mentioned in my own book about him, his children return to childhood, but they do so gaining rather than losing control of themselves and their world, and Maurice seems to suggest that children who aren't made to feel ashamed of themselves will discover an innate goodness and won't really need to be policed. Yet he thought that culture can cohere and still allow for the expression of uncivilized, primary-process kinds of desires and behaviors."

"How do you think Sendak applied these notions to his children's books?"

"Maurice's great insight has to do with his understanding that childhood is its own battleground, a testing place where you refuse to behave and can scream at your mother—'I'm going to eat you up, Mom!'—and get sent to bed and then flee and go to where the wild things are and then come back and you're not rejected for being a barbarian."

"Don't you think that Sendak and Dr. Seuss were on the same page with regard to these issues?"

"Maurice revered Dr. Seuss," Kushner told me, "and these two guys are sort of saying, We don't have to pretend that children are these little tightly screwed together, Victorian kewpie-doll things. But it's an unfair rap to say that Maurice and Dr. Seuss created the anarchy of the sixties by telling kids that it's okay to be hell-raisers, because in fact that was boiling away under the surface of American culture way before then."

"The Brownies and the Goops were early-twentieth-century trouble-makers," I pointed out.

"Right, and then there were the Katzenjammer Kids and even Mickey Mouse. Maurice loved Mickey in the 1930s, before he became Gene Kelly."

"I recall that Sendak bemoaned the fact that Mickey became a suburbanite and abandoned his street friends."

"They turned him into a butch little mouse when he's actually more of a rat!" Kushner remarked, laughing. "But the point is that Maurice's and Dr. Seuss's kids always return to civilized order. And that's an important thing, because we don't want to have a radical rejection of human connection. We want to live in a nonparalyzed, nonstatic way, but you can have dynamism and security at the same time. And that's what we were saying before about hiding and then being found—you have to be able to go to insane places and then come back. And that's what a lot of Maurice's stories are about."

"But isn't it important," I asked, "to have parents who will allow you to go to those places?"

"Yes, you need parents who will help you journey into those places, parents who are not going to *not* read you *Outside Over There,* who are going to let you go through Ida's journey and will be there to make sure you're not too scared. And at the end you'll be back home, but now as a person who understands these mysterious things as being a part of life's meaning and life's purpose and life's beauty and tragedy. And having fully plunged into the labyrinth, you develop a kind of cooling distance from these things and attain a kind of mastery over them. Which also speaks to what we were talking about before with regard to Maurice's admiration for the classic form of giving yourself a very narrow set of circumstances to work from, then digging deep and making the limitation part of the strength—and that's what growing up is."

"In your book about Sendak," I reminded Kushner, "you wrote that when you first visited him in Connecticut, he recounted to you this absolutely incredible story about how when he was about three years old and suffering from one of his frequent childhood illnesses, his mother, Sadie, apparently came into his room and swore that she saw him standing up in his crib and talking in Yiddish to a photographic portrait of his deceased maternal grandfather, Reb Moishe Schindler, that was hanging on the wall. Sadie thought that her father was trying to persuade Maurice to come into the *yenne welt*—the land of the dead—and that Maurice was trying to climb into the picture."

"Yes," said Kushner, "and she ripped the portrait from the wall and tore it into pieces."

"But then you mentioned that almost forty years later, after his mother died, Sendak, his brother, Jack, and his sister, Natalie, were going through her closets and discovered those pieces stuffed into a wad of tissue paper."

"I mean, Sadie loved Maurice," Kushner explained, "and she destroyed her father's picture in order to save her son, but even though she had been told to get rid of those fragments, she couldn't do it, because Reb Schindler was her father."

"And you also mentioned that Sendak then had those fragments reas-

Maurice Sendak's maternal grandfather, Reb Moishe Schindler. This is the original photo portrait that Sendak had restored after his mother, Sadie, tore it to pieces when Sendak was a child.

sembled by a specialist from the Metropolitan Museum. So his re-collecting of those fragments," I suggested, "really seems to have been a loving act of kindness on his part, as well as a kind of re-remembering."

"It was *so* Maurice," Kushner said, "because given that his grandfather was, after all, going to take over his soul, he nevertheless framed the portrait and hung it over his bed. So it was an act of kindness, but at the same time I think there was also a kind of death desire in that, as if Maurice were saying to his grandfather, You should have taken me from this world of pain years ago, and now I want you to come back and get me. You didn't take me the first time, and now it's time."

"There's a medieval French song called 'My End Is My Beginning,'" I told Kushner, "and to end our conversation I thought we could circle back to Herman Melville, because if not for him you might not have met Sendak."

"I might not have."

"When I myself first met Sendak, in 1976," I said, "he explained to me that what fascinated him most about Melville was the two levels of his writing, one visible and the other invisible, and he added, 'As far down as the whale goes in the water is as deep as Herman writes.' He felt that this was also true of Melville's early novel *Redburn,* and when I asked him what there was about that book that moved him so much, he said it all had to do with a walk that Redburn takes in the English countryside, and declared, 'There's a mystery there, a clue, a nut, a bolt, and if I put it together, I find me.' I was wondering if you ever read that novel."

"I've read almost everything Melville wrote," Kushner told me, "but I don't remember the details of Redburn's walk."

"I myself read it in college, but I didn't remember those details either, so after Sendak spoke to me about it I reread the book, and in the chapter about Redburn's walk, Melville describes a pastoral setting of green hedges, charming little dales, and cottages embosomed in honeysuckle, and when Redburn comes to a green bank shaded by an old tree, in a moment of ecstasy he throws himself down on the green grass under the tree."

"And that walk in the countryside," Kushner recalled, "takes place after Redburn previously took a terrifying walk through Liverpool, where he saw starving, half-dead people lying in the street. As for Maurice, I think that in order for him to survive, he eventually had to leave New York—it's the passage from the city into the natural world, a Brooklyn kid who moves to the Connecticut woods—and he then spent his life looking at the beautiful trees that grew all around him. Maurice didn't *own* those trees, but he felt he was their guest, and he revered them."

"It reminds me of the English poet Andrew Marvell's famous lines 'Annihilating all that's made / To a green thought in a green shade.'"

"Yes, that's exquisite," Kushner said.

"What do you think Sendak might have meant when he remarked that in *Redburn* he found himself?"

"You know, Maurice had a heart attack when he visited the English countryside in 1967," Kushner informed me, "and I think that after that he began to find in the natural world something sublime and godlike and a kind of nonhuman beauty that in a way somehow excused human wickedness. And I think that along with an intimation of his own mortality, Maurice also experienced a sense of the eternal."

"It sounds," I said, "as if that moment of crisis coincided with Sendak's newfound love for England."

"Yes, I do think that Maurice felt some kind of Eden, some kind of paradise in England. He loved the poetry of Keats, which is so full of beautiful flower, fruit, and tree images. Keats was one of his heroes, and he even kept a death mask of Keats at the foot of his bed.

John Keats's death mask in Maurice Sendak's home. *Photo by Lynn Caponera*

And he loved Shakespeare's *The Winter's Tale* and the old English Christmas carol 'In the Bleak Midwinter,' based on a poem by Christina Rossetti, with its lines 'In the bleak midwinter, frosty wind made moan, / Earth stood hard as iron, water like a stone.' But unlike a lot of stupid Americans who are infatuated with kings, queens, and princes, Maurice's attachment was to the kind of paradise that William Blake assures us England was before the Industrial Revolution."

"When Sendak refers to 'a clue, a nut, and a bolt,' what do you think he might have meant?"

"I think it was that powerful yearning for a lost paradise, and I think that that's what Melville is writing about in *Redburn*—you go from Dante's City of Dis to the garden."

"To the green thought in the green shade," I suggested.

"That's right," said Kushner. "During the last three or four years of his life, Maurice found it horribly difficult to come into the city—he hated it, and it pained him every time the Christmas tree in Rockefeller Center went up. I would take a picture of it and send to him just to tease him, and he'd rant, 'Those bastards, why did they do that, it's murder, I'll cut it down and stick those stupid lights . . .' He was half kidding, but he also half meant it. And I think that what Maurice was ultimately getting at when he talked about the clue, the nut, and the bolt was his feeling that there finally *is* some place, there *is* some paradise, that we can return to."

Afterword

Vladimir Nabokov once referred to his "never-resolved childhood."

For his part, Maurice Sendak confessed, "I still have an unruly four-

year-old in me," and as he confirmed to PBS's Jeffrey Brown, "There's

probably more child living in me than adult, and that is not a Peter

Pan thought at all, because it's quite hurtful and strange. There are

two perceptions: you know that you're an adult and act as much as you

can like an adult, but you're also driven by something else internally

which is riotous and strange, which we call *the kid*." Sendak acknowl-

edged that he had had a very tough time as a kid. "I had the courage to explore intense loneliness and anger in my childhood," he once remarked, "and I recall its emotional upsurges—which is something nonverbal—and I then had to find the form and shape with which to express them." And it was in the indelible children's books that he created as an adult that he gave those upsurges, in Shakespeare's words, "a local habitation and a name."

In books like *Kenny's Window, Pierre, The Sign on Rosie's Door, Where the Wild Things Are,* and *Outside Over There,* Sendak evinced a rare and preternatural ability to convey and depict with visual and verbal incandescence the anger, fears, loneliness, vulnerabilities, and frustrations of childhood; and he always abjured what he considered to be mawkish and saccharine children's books, with what he called their "never-ending ring-around-the-rosie-let's-make-the-world-a-happy-easy-frustrationless-place-for-the-kids" attitude, which he believed were published under false colors because they served only to indulge grown-ups' often sentimental recollections of their own childhoods. But as he admitted in his 1964 Caldecott Medal acceptance speech, "Of course, we must avoid frightening children, if by that we mean protecting them from experiences beyond their emotional capabilities, but I doubt that this is what most people mean when they say 'We must not frighten children.' The need for evasive books is the most obvious indication of the common wish to protect children from their everyday fears and anxieties, a hopeless wish that denies the child's endless battle with disturbing emotions."

But as Sendak also admitted, "I do not deny that a somber element colors my vision of childhood. I reject the implication that this is not a true vision . . . but we know that childhood is a marvelous time as well—perhaps even the best time of all." Of all children's-book creators, it seems to me that Sendak most daringly and rapturously summoned up remembrances of unrepressed and untrammeled childhood bliss, as he did in his depictions of children flying naked in their dreams, most indelibly little Mickey floating

out of his clothes into the Night Kitchen, wallowing in dough, and bathing sensuously in his elixir of milk. "It was all paradise," Sendak told me when we first met in 1976. "We all once lived in the Garden of Eden, and as we grew up we no longer did. That's what growing up is all about—we have to grow up—but that doesn't mean we must or should forget what that minute of pleasure was all about."

One of Sendak's heroes, Herman Melville, similarly conveyed a sense of this paradisal state, but also extended its possibilities to include a more communal and all-embracing joyousness that did not lose touch with the instinctual forces of childhood. In an astonishing scene in *Moby-Dick,* Melville described Ishmael sitting on the deck of the *Pequod* and joining his comrades in squeezing lumps of whale sperm into fluid. "I squeezed that sperm till I myself almost melted into it," Ishmael tells us. "I squeezed that sperm till a strange sort of insanity came over me; and I found myself unwittingly squeezing my co-laborers' hands in it, mistaking their hands for the gentle globules. Such an abounding, affectionate, friendly, loving feeling did this avocation beget that at last I was continually squeezing their hands, and looking up into their eyes sentimentally, as much as to say,—Oh! my dear fellow beings, why should we longer cherish any social acerbities, or know the slightest ill humor or envy! Come; let us squeeze hands all round; nay, let us squeeze ourselves into each other; let us squeeze ourselves universally into the very milk and sperm of kindness."

"I'M AN ARTIST who does books that are apparently more appropriate for children than for anyone else," Maurice Sendak once remarked to me, "but I never set *out* to do books for children—I *do* books for children, but I don't know why." Asked by Stephen Colbert in a January 2012 interview why he wrote for children, Sendak replied, "I *don't* write for children." "You don't?" said Colbert, feigning incredulity. "No," Sendak replied, "I write a book, and somebody says, '*That's* for children!'" But in an informal talk he gave in Philadelphia in 1985, he confessed, "Despite the fact that I don't write with children in mind, I long ago discovered that they make the best audience. They certainly make the best critics. They are more candid and to the point than professional critics. Of course, almost anybody is. But when children love your book, it's 'I love your book, thank you, I want to marry you when I grow up.' Or it's 'Dear Mr. Sendak: I hate your book. Hope you die soon. Cordially.'"

Sendak would furthermore always make a distinction between "authors who write *consciously* for children, and those who *have* to write"—a notion he shared with P. L. Travers, the creator of Mary Poppins, who declared, "You do not chop off a section of your imaginative substance and make a book specifically for children, for—if you are honest—you have no idea where childhood ends and maturity begins. It is all endless and all one." Similarly, Melville himself wrote: "Who in the rainbow can draw the line where the violet tint ends and the orange tint begins? Distinctly we see the difference of the colors, but where exactly does the one first blendingly enter into the other? So with sanity and insanity." And one might also add, "So with childhood and adulthood."

"The greatest writers, like the greatest illustrators, for children," Sendak reminded me, "are those who draw upon their child sources, their dream sources—they don't forget them. There's William Blake and George MacDonald, and there's Dickens. I've often said that there's a peculiar charm of being in a room in a Dickens novel, where the furniture and the saucepans are alive, where chairs move, where every inanimate object has a personality. Dickens sees and hears as children do, the way they endow everything with life.

"And then there's Henry James, whom I would call a children's-book writer—why not? He would have dropped dead if you had said that to him, but his all-absorbing interest in children and their relationships to adults creates some of his greatest stories—just the way he allows children to stay up and see what the grown-ups are really doing. In *What Maisie Knew,* children are constantly mixing in the most deranged adult society, and they're permitted to view and morally judge their elders. It's like a fantasy come true. It's like Mickey not wanting to go to sleep in order to see what goes on in the Night Kitchen, and James's children stay up at night too. Maisie hardly says anything, but we all know what she knows, and we see her know it. It's incredible how children are victimized in James, but are morally so strong."

For Sendak, nowhere was this moral strength more powerfully and hauntingly depicted than in the primal tales of the Brothers Grimm. "A story like 'Little Brother, Little Sister' or 'Snow White' says everything in metaphor," he explained, "and it's something we've always known about fairy tales—they talk about incest, the Oedipus complex, about psychotic mothers who throw their children out. They tell things about life which children know instinctively, and the pleasure and relief lie in finding these things expressed in language that children can live with. You can't eradicate these feelings—they exist and they're a great source of creative inspiration."

He considered "Hansel and Gretel" to be "the toughest story in the world," compared it to "a fist right in the face," and observed, "People are afraid of it, yet it's famous because it's so truthful. Hansel and Gretel are to me the most heroic of the Grimms' children, but the story is really about Gretel, because she's the cool-headed one, she figures out how to save herself and her brother." And with Ida, who saves her baby sister in *Outside Over There,* Sendak created another one of children's literature's most intrepid child heroines. "The subject of all of my own work from the very beginning," he stated, "has been, to put it simply, the extraordinary heroism of children in the face of having to live in a mostly indifferent adult world," and he would famously declare, "The one question I am obsessed with is, how do children survive?"

Sendak's answer to this question, suggested Dr. Richard Gottlieb, was that children survive when they exercise their creative imagination, and Gottlieb pointed to Sendak's assertion that "it is through fantasy that children achieve catharsis—it is the best means they have for taming wild things." And what enabled Sendak himself to survive was his own creative work, which, he acknowledged, "miraculously kept me alive and kept me employed. That's who I am, that's how I live, that's how I protect myself." As he told the filmmakers Lance Bangs and Spike Jonze, "Sitting down at a drawing table, turning on the radio, and making pictures—it's sublime, and it's where all of your weaknesses of character and all the blemishes of your personality end. You're doing the one thing you want to do, and you do it well, and at that moment I feel that I'm a lucky man."

But in his struggle to create *Outside Over There,* Sendak informed me that he had suffered a devastating emotional breakdown, describing the experience as one of "falling off a ladder that goes down deep into the unconscious," and I was reminded of little Pip jumping overboard in *Moby-Dick.* Herman Melville had written: "The sea had jeeringly kept his finite body up, but drowned the infinite of his soul. Not drowned entirely, though. Rather carried down alive to wondrous depths, where strange shapes of the unwarped primal world glided to and fro before his passive eyes; and the miser-merman, Wisdom, revealed his hoarded heaps."

When Sendak first spoke to me about his breakdown, he characterized it as a kind of death-and-rebirth experience, one from which he had miraculously emerged with the most treasured of his books. I quoted to him Jesus's saying: "And whosoever will lose his life for my sake shall find it," and he responded, "That's basically it. You have to take the risk of dying. That's the beautiful point of it all, and in a sense, that's also the moral of *Outside Over There.*"

"That certainly isn't the typical moral one finds in the typical children's picture book," I pointed out.

"Well, it depends on what you're looking for when you're doing a picture book," Sendak said. "I'm looking for salvation. Aren't we all looking for salvation? I mean, why else do you work? Why else do you live? What purpose is there for doing anything if you're not looking for salvation?"

"What do you take salvation to mean?" I asked him.

"I'm not going to try to define what that word means, because it will be different for everybody," he replied. "But in a way I've come to know what it is. There's a look on Ida's face on the second to last page of *Outside Over There,* where she's standing next to her mother, that looks exactly like how I feel after many troubled years. It's a look of reconciliation, and it's an expression that says, This is what it is.

"In a way, it's also Judy Garland's expression at the end of *The Wizard of Oz,* when she says 'There's no place like home.' There's something terribly platitudinous about that, but wonderfully so, because just previously to her having said that, she has tried vainly to convey genuine feeling to the people around her and they won't listen to her at all. 'No, Dorothy,' they say, 'you only had a dream. No, Dorothy. No, Dorothy.' And poor Dorothy can't tell them that she's been on a terrific death trip. They just don't want to hear about that, and when she realizes that they don't want to hear about that, she says, 'There's no place like home.'

"And what an irony! Because what she's saying is, Home is where no one can ever be honest with you . . . but in fact there *is* no other place to go to. So there's no place like home. And so then what are you going to do? If you try to solve it by going someplace else, the only thing you'll come back with is the knowledge that you only have to stay where you are. The solution lies within yourself, wherever you are."

And as Maurice Sendak once declared, "When Ida goes home, I go home too."

Acknowledgments

There's a Mystery There would never have become a reality without the cooperation of the Maurice Sendak Foundation, whose board members are Lynn Caponera, Michael di Capua, Donald A. Hamburg, Spike Jonze, Dona Ann McAdams, and John Vitale. In particular, I want to express my profound gratitude to Lynn Caponera, the president of the foundation, and to Michael di Capua, who was Maurice Sendak's editor for fifty years, for their unflagging encouragement, unstinting assistance, and for giving me carte blanche to fulfill my long-harbored dream of writing a book about Maurice Sendak's *Outside Over There* in the context of this great artist's life and work.

I am also inestimably grateful to the psychoanalyst Dr. Richard M. Gottlieb, the Jungian analyst Margaret Klenck, the art historian Jane Doonan, and the playwright Tony Kushner for the countless hours they spent with me delving into, exploring, and illuminating the complex and manifold psychological, visual, and literary mysteries of *There's a Mystery There*. It was truly an honor and a privilege for me to have had the opportunity to meet and keep company with these four extraordinary people.

At Doubleday, I am especially indebted and extremely grateful to my editor, Gerald Howard, who masterfully and painstakingly gathered and wove together the myriad, diverse, and complex design and production strands of my book; and I would like to acknowledge the following gifted people who worked tirelessly on this project: the editorial production manager, Bette Alexander; the interior designer, Maria Carella; the production manager, Lorraine Hyland; and the cover designer, Michael Windsor. Thanks also to Josh Zajdman for providing invaluable assistance. And I would like to express my great appreciation to my copy editor, Liz Duvall.

For their generous help, I thank Sarah Bertalan, Denise Egielski, and Jodi Peckman.

I am deeply grateful to the poet Coleman Barks for permitting me to reprint his candent translation of Rumi's poem that begins "The breeze at dawn has secrets to tell you" and to Nancy Crampton for allowing me to use her joyous and iconic photograph of Maurice Sendak.

For their abiding generosity and support, I give heartfelt thanks to Annie Druyan, Elizabeth Garnsey, Richard Gere, Philippe Goldin, Hope Malkan, and Uma Thurman.

I also want to thank both Sonny Mehta and Jann Wenner, who first published my work over a half century ago.

And I want to express my immeasurable gratitude to my literary agent, Michael V. Carlisle.

A Note on Sources

Maurice Sendak was a preternaturally self-aware artist who was not only acutely cognizant of the childhood origins of his psychological fantasies and obsessions but also unabashedly willing to share his understanding of them in the many revelatory and forthright print, radio, television, and film interviews that he gave throughout his life.

For me, the most valuable of the print interviews were the ones he gave to the writer Nat Hentoff, whose profile of Sendak, entitled "Among Wild Things," appeared in the January 22, 1966, issue of *The New Yorker*; to the librarian Virginia Haviland, whose conversation with him at the Library of Congress on November 16, 1970, was reprinted in *Quarterly Journal of the Library of Congress* 28, no. 4 (October 1971); to the children's-book historian Leonard S. Marcus, whose three interviews from 1988, 1993, and 2011 were included in his book *Show Me a Story: Why Picture Books Matter* (Somerville, MA: Candlewick, 2012); to the writer and art director Steven Heller, whose 1984 interview was included in *Innovators of American Illustration* (New York: Van Nostrand Reinhold, 1986); to the British journalist Emma Brockes, whose 2011 interview appeared in the November/December 2012 issue of *The Believer* magazine; and to the editor in chief of *The Horn Book Magazine,* Roger Sutton, in whose fascinating interview, which

appeared in the magazine's November/December 2003 issue, Sendak confesses to
his obsession with the American reality-television series *A Baby Story,* in which
babies are shown being born. "You can see the head," Sendak tells Sutton. "You
can see the baby *coming out.* I cannot get enough of that . . . it's that first moment,
the uncontrollable gesturing . . . You know, babies show us that we're really frogs:
a torso, a penis or a vagina, and then the legs bow—it's all so basic, so elemental . . . it's 'The Mystery' . . . and I have to see it night after night."

Among the most notable of his film and television interviews were the ones he
gave to Bill Moyers on his PBS program *Now* on March 12, 2004; to Lance Bangs
and Spike Jonze in their 2009 television documentary film *Tell Them Anything You
Want: A Portrait of Maurice Sendak*; to Stephen Colbert on *The Colbert Report,* in
which Sendak wittily and wryly parries with Colbert in a now-legendary two-
part conversation that was broadcast on January 25–26, 2012 (four months before
Sendak's death), that was viewed at the time by close to a million people, and that
later went viral; and to Terry Gross, who interviewed Sendak four times on her
radio program *Fresh Air* from 1986 to 2011. The most memorable of these interviews, which took place on September 20, 2011, revealed Sendak in a profoundly
elegiac mood. "I'm not unhappy about becoming old," he confided to her. "I'm
not unhappy at what must be. It makes me cry only when I see my friends go
before me, and life gets emptied . . . and almost certainly I'll go before you, so I
won't have to miss you . . . But you know, there's something I'm finding out as
I'm aging—that I am in love with the world. And it's a blessing to get old. It's a
blessing to find the time to do things, to listen to the music, to read the books."

There are several books that are essential to one's understanding of Sendak's
life and work. The first of these is *Caldecott & Co.: Notes on Books and Pictures,*
which consists of a collection of his essays and other writings (New York: Michael
di Capua Books/Farrar, Straus and Giroux, 1988) which range from discussions
of Victorian children's picture books and Mother Goose rhymes to homages to

Mickey Mouse and Babar the elephant, and which include his extraordinary Caldecott Medal and Hans Christian Andersen Medal acceptance speeches.

The two major biographical and critical overviews of Sendak's creative endeavors are *The Art of Maurice Sendak,* by Selma G. Lanes (New York: Abrams, 1980), and *The Art of Maurice Sendak: 1980 to the Present* by Tony Kushner (New York: Abrams, 2003). Both are lavishly produced coffee-table books that, in addition to their discerning texts, which draw on the authors' conversations with Sendak, contain hundreds of full-color and black-and-white illustrations, sketches, preliminary drawings, and photographs, as well as artwork for numerous posters and book and CD covers; Kushner's book reproduces a myriad of fascinating illustrations, watercolor studies, and storyboards for the sets and costume designs that Sendak created for the many opera, theatrical, and dance productions he worked on during the last thirty years of his life. In addition to these two books, a full-color catalogue of more than two hundred Sendak artworks that were exhibited at the Society of Illustrators in New York City in 2013 was published as a book entitled *Maurice Sendak: A Celebration of the Artist and His Work* (New York: Abrams, 2013) and includes essays and reminiscences by writers, colleagues, and collaborators such as Frank Corsaro, Iona Opie, and Leonard S. Marcus. And one must importantly also mention *Angels and Wild Things: The Archetypal Poetics of Maurice Sendak,* by the children's-book scholar John Cech (University Park: Pennsylvania State University Press, 1996; new paperback edition 2013), a perspicacious and often profound literary, historical, cultural, and psychological analysis of Sendak's major children's books.

My own book has as its primary focus *Outside Over There,* which, as Sendak frequently asserted to interviewers, was the favorite of his books and the one he considered to be his masterpiece. In the May 30, 1981, issue of *The Nation,* the former director of the National Center for the Study of Children's Literature, Jerry Griswold, concurred, declaring it to be "Sendak's best work by far" and "the one which marks the apogee of the picture book form." Writing in the May 18, 1981, issue of *Newsweek,* Walter Clemons described it as "a subtle, delicate, unclassifiable work . . . that moves through dread and unadmitted hostility to sureness and beautifully serene control"—a notion that was echoed by the novelist John Gardner in the April 26, 1981, issue of *The New York Times Book Review,* in which he wrote that *Outside Over There* was a profound work of art that allowed children to "muse on . . . without fear . . . the guilt and insecurity that is the dual bane of every child's existence . . . and escape triumphant."

Several extensive analyses of *Outside Over There* have appeared in books and journals since it was first published in 1981, and three of them are indispensable. The first is the essay "Maurice Sendak's Trilogy: Disappointment, Fury, and Their Transformation Through Art," by the psychoanalyst Richard M. Gottlieb, which is included in *The Psychoanalytic Study of the Child,* vol. 63 (New Haven: Yale University Press, 2008). The second is the essay "A Picture Equals How Many Words? Narrative Theory and Picture Books for Children," by the book publisher Stephen Roxburgh, which appeared in the American children's-literature journal *The Lion and the Unicorn* 7/8 (1983–1984). And the third is the two-part essay "*Outside Over There*: A Journey in Style" which appeared in the British children's journal *Signal,* nos. 50 and 51 (May and September 1986), by the art historian Jane Doonan, in which she explores and decodes the book's visual grammar in the context of its cultural and psychological framework. Doonan is also the author of *Looking at Pictures in Picture Books* (Stroud, Gloucestershire: The Thimble Press, 1993), a compendious and insightful work in which she considers the picture book as an aesthetic object as well as a visual language, and provides illuminating examples of her analytic approach.

For his part, Maurice Sendak spoke at length to me about *Outside Over There* on April 6, 1981, one month before its official publication date, and this discussion appeared for the first time in my book *Pipers at the Gates of Dawn: The Wisdom of*

Children's Literature (New York: Random House, 1983). An expanded and now complete version of that discussion is included in *There's a Mystery There,* as is an expanded version of my 1976 interview-profile of Sendak, which was published in the December 30, 1976, issue of *Rolling Stone* magazine. Sendak also spoke at length about *Outside Over There* at a two-day conference devoted to his work at the University of California, Berkeley, in February 1996; the other participants were the Renaissance scholar Stephen Greenblatt, the music scholar Wye Allanbrook, and the psychiatrist Herbert Schreier. The proceedings from the conference's two panel discussions were published in a sixty-two-page booklet entitled *Changelings* (Townsend Center Occasional Papers, Berkeley: University of California, 1996). Sendak's extensive remarks about *Outside Over There* and the open discussions that followed those remarks were especially useful to me when I was writing *There's a Mystery There.*

Also useful to me was the Japanese novel *The Changeling,* by the Nobel Prize laureate Kenzaburo Oe, in which the Berkeley *Changelings* booklet makes a surprising appearance. The protagonist of Oe's roman à clef, which was published in Japan in 2000 and in an English translation in 2010, is an eminent Japanese writer whom Oe calls Kogito Choko but who is in fact a surrogate for Oe himself. Kogito informs us that when he was attending a conference at the Institute for Advanced Research in Berlin, he received a copy of the *Changelings* booklet from an academic who had participated in the Sendak conference in Berkeley. (Stephen Greenblatt confirmed to me that he gave Oe a copy of that booklet.) Kogito also mentions that while he was in Berlin he serendipitously came across and obtained a copy of *Outside Over There* and brought it back home to Japan.

Kogito's wife, Chikashi, becomes obsessed by Sendak's picture book and reads it as if it were actually the story of her own childhood and family; she sees her own mother in Ida's mother and declares, "This girl in the book, this Ida— she's me!" It is through Chikashi's eyes that Oe beautifully observes and analyzes in detail the images and words of *Outside Over There,* explaining to Chikashi that "the secret of life and death isn't in the bright heavens above; it's hidden in the subterranean darkness. That's why it's a mistake to fly looking up. You have to fly looking down or else you won't be able to observe the chthonic secrets." For Kenzaburo Oe, this is the ultimate mystery that exists at the heart of Maurice Sendak's masterpiece.

Illustration Credits